Why Does the Pedlar Sing?

Why Does the Pedlar Sing?

What Creativity Really Means in Advertising

PAUL FELDWICK

Matador
9 Priory Business Park,
Wistow Road, Kibworth Beauchamp,
Leicestershire. LE8 0RX
Tel: 0116 279 2299
Email: books@troubador.co.uk
Web: www.troubador.co.uk/matador
Twitter: @matadorbooks

ISBN 978 1800462 526

British Library Cataloguing in Publication Data.
A catalogue record for this book is available from the British Library.

Printed and bound in the UK by TJ Books LTD, Padstow, Cornwall
Typeset in 11pt Adobe Jenson Pro by Troubador Publishing Ltd, Leicester, UK

Matador is an imprint of Troubador Publishing Ltd

O master! If you did but hear the pedlar at the door, you would never dance again after a tabor and pipe; no, the bagpipe could not move you: he sings several tunes, faster than you'll tell money: he utters them as he had eaten ballads, and all men's ears grow to his tunes…

SHAKESPEARE, *THE WINTER'S TALE*, ACT IV

Also by Paul Feldwick

The Anatomy of Humbug

Fascinating and superbly written. It takes us from the beginning of the modern era of advertising up to the present, with charming anecdotes and intelligent analyses of the people and ideas that have made us the struggling, bewildered ad hacks we are today.

Bob Hoffman, author of *Advertising for Skeptics*

No-one has previously discussed the various "practitioner theories" of advertising so comprehensively. It's a great story, and I learned a lot.

Patrick Barwise, Emeritus Professor of Management and Marketing, London Business School.

An elegant overview of the history of advertising theory, with the added joy of being filtered through the immense wisdom, experience and brain of this advertising guru.

Tess Alps, former Chair, Thinkbox

A thoughtful and beautifully written reflection on the history of advertising practice.

Nigel Hollis, author of *Brand Premium* and former Chief Global Analyst, Millward Brown

The Anatomy of Humbug: How to Think Differently About Advertising is available from Matador as hardback, ebook, and audiobook.

Contents

Preface

A Serious Business?

Advertising is a serious business, and advertisers spend serious money investing in it. Yet from the earliest times, much advertising has been far from serious in its appearance, featuring song and dance, celebrities, cartoons, talking animals, childish jingles, low humour, and all the other tropes of popular culture.

Indeed, its vulgarity has often offended commentators as much as its questionable morals. The Austrian economist, Ludwig von Mises, was a stalwart defender of the freedom to advertise, yet he believed that

> Like all things designed to suit the taste of the masses, advertising is repellent
> to people of delicate feeling.

Sadly, those 'people of delicate feeling' have often included not just advertising's critics, but many of its own clients, and even quite a few in the ad agencies themselves. Embarrassed by advertising's all-too-obvious and inescapable links with popular culture, they have constructed for it an alternative persona – advertising as an honest salesman, which offers its audiences only sober facts and rational benefits.

This is not wrong, but it only represents a part of what advertising does – and perhaps not even the most important part. For many years, this double-think made it harder than it need have been to produce effective advertising; but it did not make it totally impossible. I worked for thirty years in an agency where we repeatedly succeeded in smuggling a cast of dancing polar bears, laughing aliens and singing chimpanzees past the barriers of selling propositions, consumer benefits and reasons why.

Today we probably understand the psychology behind the apparent fluff and nonsense of advertising better than ever before. Concepts like 'mental availability' and the 'affect heuristic', the largely unconscious nature of mental associative networks, the importance of the right brain hemisphere in connecting emotions, images, and memory, all these (as we shall see) begin to explain why puppies, clowns, or monkeys on bicycles create liking and fame, which are what build valuable brands. Thanks to the published research of Byron Sharp and Jenni Romaniuk, Peter Field and Les Binet, Orlando Wood, Robert Heath and others, we know the importance of stories, emotions, slogans, music, and distinctive brand assets in making advertising that works.

All the more odd, then, that so many of today's ad agencies and their clients appear to ignore all this, or even to do the exact opposite. While more money is spent on advertising worldwide than ever before, there's evidence that it is now less effective, and more disliked by the public, than it has ever been. Thirty years ago, a majority of the British public agreed that 'Sometimes the ads are better than the programmes' – the proportion who agree with that today is vanishingly small. Instead, the vast majority of the younger generation now deliberately avoid any exposure to advertising at all.

There will be those who object that the world has changed. That today's techniques of individual targeting and personalisation in the digital space have superseded the old analogue needs to be engaging, entertaining, or memorable. But the reality is that, while the internet has transformed so many aspects of our lives and our commerce, it will never transform the fundamental psychology behind advertising and brands. Jeff Bezos knew, when he started Amazon, that

'Brand names are more important on-line than they are in the physical world'; the most important search engine remains the one in your head. Meanwhile, those who fail to understand how humans actually make choices will go on wasting immense sums of money on the emperor's new clothes.

So while advertising today has access to a wider range of communication channels than ever before, it is failing to make the best use of any of them. This is because there seems to be a greater gap than ever between our emerging theoretical understanding of advertising, and the cultural beliefs and fashions that direct the way it is actually produced.

This book is an attempt to bridge that gap. My intention is not just to review what we know today about how advertising works, but to illustrate its truth and bring it to life through stories and examples from advertising and brand history, including some from my own experience. I want to remind us all what so much successful advertising of the past actually looked and sounded like, to reflect on the processes and conditions that made it possible to create that kind of work, and to inspire advertisers and their agencies to adapt the same principles to the changed media landscape of today. I would like to encourage all those who work in advertising and brand management to suspend their 'delicate feelings' about what really creates popularity and fame, and to embrace the idea that advertising is at least as much showmanship as it is salesmanship.

Advertising is a serious business. So the advertisers who invest their money in it should pay attention to the fundamentals of how it works, not to what is fashionable or novel. It is time to rediscover the fact that advertising builds brands best when it is entertaining, popular and memorable, when it is not just a pitch, but a performance.

It is time for the Pedlar to sing again. It would be good for business, and less annoying for the public. It could even be fun.

Part One

The Pedlar At The Door

Then I said, 'You sing and so advertise your trade?'

He answered, 'I do. It lifts the heart, it shortens the way, it attracts the attention of the citizens, it guarantees good work'.

HILAIRE BELLOC, *HILLS AND THE SEA*

'Only a singer you say, Mr Norman. Well, I want you to know that the Beautee Soap Company thinks singers are mighty important. And I'll tell you why, Mr Norman.'

He opened the drawer of the table and triumphantly held aloft a bar of Beautee Soap.

'Because singers can sell soap, Mr Norman. Right, Kimberley?'

'RIGHT,' said Kimberley.

FREDERICK WAKEMAN, *THE HUCKSTERS*

Don't *sing* your selling message. Selling is a serious business.

DAVID OGILVY, *CONFESSIONS OF AN ADVERTISING MAN*

Chapter One
Richard Latham's Rug

If you lived in the UK during the 1990s you may well remember a long-running Barclaycard campaign, a series of TV commercials in which Rowan Atkinson played an arrogant but incompetent secret agent called Richard Latham.

Latham – an early foreshadowing of Atkinson's later creation, Johnny English – was always accompanied by a naive assistant called Bough (pronounced 'Boff'). In the opening commercial, Latham was issued with a Barclaycard as part of his equipment, but in his many subsequent adventures he persistently refused to use it. The outcome was always that Latham was made to look foolish, while Bough, who did use his Barclaycard, ended up appearing to be the clever one. The films were shot on locations around the world, they had high production values, and were very funny.

In one of the best known ads, Latham and Bough are buying rugs in a souk, somewhere in North Africa (the commercial was actually filmed in Cairo). Bough produces his Barclaycard. 'A Barclaycard? Put it away, Bough,' says Latham. 'The Touareg are an ancient people. They understand only hard cash and hard bargaining.' He then tries to haggle in some language which is equally incomprehensible to us and to the carpet seller. 'You sound fluent, sir', says Bough. 'We are both fluent, Bough,' says Latham tetchily, 'Sadly, in different languages. HOW MUCH IS THE RUG?'. The pair leave the bazaar, each with a rug on his shoulder. 'So, where did your Barclaycard get you?' asks Latham. 'Well, it got me rug insured for three months', says Bough. 'Insurance, Bough?' says Latham contemptuously, 'I think I can handle a rug!' As he says this he swings round, and the end of his rug behind him catches fire on an open flame. Neither of them notices that his rug is blazing fiercely as they walk away into the sunset. 'Ah, smell those Touareg camp fires!' says Latham, 'Unmistakeable!' A local boy runs after them shouting an alarm but Latham takes him for a beggar and tells him to 'push off'.

It takes longer to describe than to watch, and I haven't even included all the dialogue – it's an object lesson in how much story and how much humour can be skilfully included in sixty seconds of film. At the time of writing, it's easy to find all the commercials on YouTube, so if you're curious you can look them up; no description does them justice.

I worked on this campaign, so you might expect me to be biased in its favour. But we need to start by establishing that the campaign did more than just entertain. In 1996, the Rowan Atkinson Barclaycard campaign won a Gold in the IPA Advertising Effectiveness Awards, a prize given not for film-making skills, but for demonstrating to a critical jury of experts that the advertising had made a major contribution to Barclaycard's business success. So before we go on, let's examine what these business benefits of the campaign were.

Barclaycard had been launched in the sixties as Britain's first ever credit card, and was joined a few years later by Access, a brand owned by a consortium of major banks. During the eighties Barclaycard joined up with VISA, and Access with Mastercard, in order to get worldwide acceptance. But this also opened up the category to competition, as any operator could now create a credit card using one of the two global networks. So by 1990 there was competition from smaller banks such as TSB, 'affiliate' cards from companies like British Airways, and even from a wide range of charities. Credit cards were in danger of becoming a commodity category. And the advent of bank debit cards, in the late eighties, now made it easy to pay by card, without the need for a credit card at all.

The impact of all this on Barclaycard's business had become noticeable by 1990: it had lost share of the number of cards issued, share of turnover, numbers of new card applications, and ultimately profits. The company planned a major re-launch, and to support this decided to look for a new ad agency and campaign.

The previous campaign had featured Alan Whicker, a popular and slightly eccentric reporter and TV presenter who appeared in a range of exotic locations, demonstrating the worldwide acceptance of Barclaycard. As the worldwide acceptance was in reality a VISA property, Barclaycard no longer believed this was a strong enough claim. As part of the re-launch, they were planning (with some trepidation) to introduce for the first time an annual fee, and to justify this they were adding a range of new benefits to the card, such as free insurance on purchases, and medical assistance abroad. The Rowan Atkinson films dramatised these in different ways.

Our advertising objectives were, simply, to encourage more people to get the card, to keep the card, and to use the card more often. Over five years, all these were achieved. Numbers of new cardholders increased, most dramatically among younger people; 'churn' was reduced; and econometric modelling showed that the amount of increased turnover per card had itself more than paid for the advertising. Meanwhile, the Access brand, without consistent advertising support, rapidly declined, and the banks eventually decided to close it down. Barclaycard emerged the undisputed leader in the UK credit card sector, as it remains today.

*

I've introduced this Barclaycard campaign as a specific case, in order to explore two general questions about advertising.

The first is the question of how we think advertising works – an inquiry I began in *The Anatomy of Humbug*. What might be the connection between a rising celebrity, some humorous films set in exotic locations, and an individual choosing to pull out one card rather than another when buying a pair of shoes? The Barclaycard films were widely regarded as excellent entertainment. But what's the link between the apparently unrelated spheres of *entertainment* and *selling*?

The second is a more obviously practical question: what are the processes, practices and cultures necessary to making effective advertising? In this case, we can examine the sequence of events that led us to a successful outcome. What general principles, if any, might we learn from this process?

The answers to both sets of questions are connected, but they are not obvious.

Let's begin by thinking about how this advertising might have worked.

We know, based on the rigorous evidence of a Gold IPA paper, that this Barclaycard campaign was a success – that it made a significant contribution to the business. But by what means, psychological or otherwise, did a series of entertaining short films influence people's behaviour, on a large scale, in a field which most people would consider rather a serious one – personal finance?

In *The Anatomy of Humbug*, I described a number of ways in which practitioners have thought in general about how advertising works. I refer to these as mental models, or metaphors, or even theories (in the original Greek sense of 'ways of seeing'). Because these are different ways of trying to explain the same phenomenon, they are not mutually exclusive, and none is entirely right or wrong. However, the choice of which one we use in practice – a choice that is nearly always made unconsciously – often has important consequences for what actions we take.

So if, for example, we assume (as many often do) that advertising always works by *communicating a message*, we will insist on including a clear message in the execution, we will reject ads that don't appear to do this, and we will use research to test whether the message is being clearly transmitted, recalled and believed. If, on the other hand, we are able to take a critical stance about our assumptions, we can decide how relevant 'message transmission' is to what we think we are doing, and whether other models or theories might be more important to guide our decision making.

Let's review some possible hypotheses about how this Barclaycard campaign achieved its results, using some of the 'models' I outlined in *The Anatomy of Humbug*.

1.   The Salesmanship model

I named this model from a famous early definition of advertising as 'salesmanship in print'. Its first proponent, a copywriter called John E. Kennedy, argued that, as in face to face selling, advertising needs to persuade by giving a 'reason why' – factual information about why the product is to be preferred. It's a model of rational persuasion, requiring that the advertiser first gains the conscious attention of the audience, and then delivers the persuasive 'sales message'.

Later, others added the idea that the sales message should be simple enough to be lodged in the memory, as in Rosser Reeves's updated (and upper case) 1961 version of 'salesmanship in print' for the TV era:

ADVERTISING IS THE ART OF GETTING A UNIQUE SELLING PROPOSITION INTO THE HEADS OF THE MOST PEOPLE AT THE LOWEST POSSIBLE COST

In many ways this has remained through the decades the dominant mental model of advertising effect. It is the one most often articulated, and the one that has most influenced decision making, creative briefing, and research methods.

It is not surprising, then, that many advertising and marketing people, when asked to explain the Barclaycard campaign, automatically focus first on the messages or product benefits contained in it. There were a number of added value services included in the re-launch, such as free insurance, medical assistance, and rapid replacement of lost cards, and all these are dramatised in the commercials. 'Cairo' is a clear example: the whole drama is a demonstration of a key benefit of using Barclaycard, the fact that it gives you three months free insurance on every purchase.

One hypothesis, then, is that this campaign was successful because it communicated a number of tangible product benefits linked to the brand – and we know from research that it did effectively achieve this. The function of the storytelling, the humour and the celebrity were merely a means to that end: they were there to *get attention* and perhaps to help lodge the sales message in the *memory*. Bill Bernbach, for instance, stressed

> ...the importance of creativity in *getting attention* to an ad and making the *product advantage memorable*...(1980: *emphasis added*)

because even he, the leader of the so-called 'creative revolution' in advertising, was fundamentally a believer in fact-based, 'selling' propositions.

Many of us are so used to thinking this way about ads, that we might be inclined to stop there. But while the transmission of the product information here seems to play a part, we could also question how important that part really is. For instance, the new product benefits had already been widely communicated to existing card users by other means, so that even before the campaign broke awareness of them was high. And if the benefits were in themselves so compelling, could they not have been communicated in a more direct and simple way? Was it really necessary to have expensive location shoots in Fiji and Cairo?

Perhaps something else might be going on here. But what?

2.   The Subconscious Associations model

A simple idea which has been around since Aristotle, was revived in the eighteenth century by Locke and Hume, and is still seen as important today by psychologists and neuroscientists, is the principle of *mental associative networks*. Our minds make sense of the world by continually building networks of associations – between things, words, concepts, sensations and feelings. Modern neuroscientists such as Damasio even have some theories about how this happens physically within the brain, so it's not just, as it once may have been, an imaginative metaphor. These associative networks are complex, continually developing and changing, and influenced by many factors including the intensity or the uniqueness of the stimuli we receive, their proximity or similarity to each other, and the frequency of their repetition.

And for the most part, our associative networks are continually under construction and reconstruction *without the involvement of our conscious minds*. Thus, for example, we might meet a stranger and at once feel vaguely in awe of him, without ever realising that his face and half-moon glasses remind us of our old headmaster. Or, a certain picture that lifts our spirits for no obvious reason may be evoking connections with particular happy times when we were young.

It would be surprising if this idea of subconscious associations wasn't relevant to advertising, and the connection was recognised as early as 1903 by Walter Dill Scott, a Psychology Professor at Northwestern University in Illinois. Scott thought advertising commonly worked by association, or as he also called it, suggestion, and that people were very often not consciously aware that they had been influenced by, or even exposed to, advertising. He noticed that he preferred washing with Ivory Soap because it seemed to him to have 'a halo of spotless elegance' about it, and he considered that this impression of his had been subconsciously induced by advertising.

This kind of thinking was sidelined in the following decades by the dominance of the 'salesmanship' school, but it surfaced again in the advertising boom of the 1950s under the name of 'motivation research'. Ernest Dichter and other quasi-Freudian researchers argued that advertising mainly influenced the mind unconsciously, through colours, images, music, connotative language and other forms of suggestion.

However, the way they presented their case invited a backlash. This was led by journalist Vance Packard, who argued that 'mass persuasion through the unconscious' constituted sinister manipulation and brainwashing, and threatened dire consequences for freedom and democracy. It was not long before the ad industry collectively decided to back off, and to reassert that they were merely honest 'salesmen' who give people plain facts and reasons why. Rosser Reeves (the man who invented the Unique Selling Proposition, or USP) assured the public that

> There are no hidden persuaders. Advertising works openly, in the bare and pitiless sunlight.

The motivation researchers may have overstated their case, and been overly fond of Freudian jargon, but, on the whole, today's scientists would generally agree they weren't far wrong. Huge advances in psychology and neuroscience in the last thirty years now indicate that most of what goes on in our minds is unconscious, and that's just how it is. If we reframe the basic idea behind this model as *mental associative networks*, we can understand how images and music experienced in an ad, and the feelings that accompany that experience, may become associated with the brand advertised – and then influence behaviour.

So, in this Barclaycard campaign, there are many things going on besides the conscious story about the product benefits. The exotic locations are not merely an indulgence, but continue to link the brand with worldwide travel, in a pleasant and aspirational way – a theme that had been already established through several years of the previous Alan Whicker advertising. While it's not a factual or conscious differentiating claim, creating a strong association between the Barclaycard brand and the idea of worldwide acceptability is enough to influence choice.

Moreover, Alan Whicker, despite his popularity, left subconscious associations of a previous era– in 1991 he was seventy years old, and his much parodied blazer and moustache were the uniform of an older generation. By contrast, the thirty-six year old Atkinson, whose fame at that time was still growing, represented youth, and a certain style of anti-establishment satire. And the ads as a whole, with their well crafted humour and high production values, evoked pleasant feelings in the audience, shifting their impressions of the brand from being a distant and slightly threatening financial institution to something more friendly and familiar.

It's likely, then, that all these subconscious associations may have contributed to the campaign's success. We know, for instance, that the ads especially led to the brand being seen as more youthful, and stimulated most new users among younger people.

But it's also possible that there's a more fundamental – and apparently simpler – principle at work.

3.   The Salience, Fame, or Mental Availability model

Byron Sharp, Jenni Romaniuk, and their colleagues at the Ehrenberg-Bass Institute, have in recent years proposed that just one factor explains most of the contribution of advertising to brand sales. This is what they call *mental availability*.

'Availability' is a concept popularised by the Nobel prizewinning psychologist and economist, Daniel Kahneman. In *Thinking Fast and Slow*, Kahneman posits two kinds of mental process – System 1, which uses 'heuristics' or short cuts to make rapid sense of the world, and System 2, which is slower and more analytic. Most of the time our minds are using System 1, so that our choices are powerfully influenced by what most easily and vividly comes to our minds, often contrary to what logic would tell us to do: for instance, many people are nervous of flying, despite the fact that statistically it is much safer than other modes, because the images we have of plane crashes are especially vivid and dramatic, and feature more often as major news stories. He has called this the *availability heuristic*, and in the world of brands it suggests that, other things being equal, we are more inclined to choose the brand that is most 'available' to our minds, because it is vivid and distinctive as well as familiar.

In everyday language, it is convenient to equate this to everyday words such as *salience* or *fame*, though Sharp and his colleagues now prefer to avoid those terms, as they can be defined in different terms to what they mean by mental availability. Mental availability is not, for instance, identical with typical research measures of 'top of mind awareness' (TOMA) or 'salience'. Such concepts normally measure salience in response to a single 'trigger' question, but mental availability is the likelihood of the brand name coming to mind in as many relevant situations as possible. It is therefore maximised by the breadth and richness of the brand's associations, not by its connection to any single trigger.

Sharp and Romaniuk explicitly found their argument in mental associative network theory, so in some ways this is a variation of the previous model: it differs in that it emphasises the strength and number of associations over their specific nature. This apparently subtle shift does, however, have major implications for the practical business of managing brands and creating advertising.

The Ehrenbergians have argued for decades (based on solid and consistent data) that brands do not generally differentiate themselves very much from each other on image or attribute ratings, despite widespread beliefs to the contrary among marketers. Brands that are more successful are simply those that have greater mental availability among more people, and therefore a greater number of people use them. But one necessary condition for high mental availability is that a brand must be uniquely *distinctive*, and not confused with others. Distinctiveness, unlike *differentiation* as it's usually understood, is not necessarily, or even usually, meaningful: indeed, Byron Sharp has coined the memorable phrase, the 'meaningless distinctive', to describe the visual, verbal, or other tangible devices that make successful brands uniquely memorable. The iconic Coca-Cola bottle, or the Nike Swoosh, for instance, don't *in themselves* 'mean' anything other than Coca-Cola or Nike, but each is powerful because it can't be mistaken for anything else and is uniquely associated with the brand. (They may appear to each of us to 'mean' a lot because, for most of us, they form part of a rich and often emotionally charged mental associative network, but these meanings are not intrinsic and may not even be intended.) These are examples of what Sharp and Romaniuk call 'distinctive brand assets': other common examples are characters (human or otherwise), slogans, and jingles.

On this basis, we could argue that this campaign contributed principally to Barclaycard's distinctiveness and mental availability. It became 'the one with Rowan Atkinson', 'the one in the bazaar', 'the one with the flaming carpet', and also 'the one with the insurance', 'the one you can use anywhere in the world', or just 'the one I saw a lot of ads for recently'. Atkinson himself quickly became a powerful distinctive asset, as did the music, a specially composed theme which recurs in all the commercials.

The 'meaning' of any of these associations is secondary to the fact that they enrich the brand's associative network, and make it more likely to seem familiar and to be thought of in purchase situations. The result is that people become more likely to apply for, keep, and use their Barclaycards (as was observed to happen), simply for these reasons.

At the risk of over-simplifying, this model suggests that the campaign grew the Barclaycard business by making Barclaycard more famous. It was thought of more often, by more people, and therefore chosen more often by more people. The entertainment, the use of the celebrity, and the unique little world that it created were all means to this end.

Yet creating fame, or mental availability, is not so simple a matter as it may at first appear. New associations are much more likely to be incorporated into our mental networks if they have some kind of emotional impact, and also if they are easily ('fluently') processed. And while there are different kinds of emotional impact, ranging from the highly pleasurable to the intensely painful, those which create a positive affect – some kind of pleasure – have two general advantages in creating fame or mental availability. Firstly, we are more likely to seek them out rather than to avoid them; and secondly, we are more likely to share them with others. If we are more likely to look at, remember and share with others things we enjoy than things we don't, then things that give us some kind of pleasure are likely to become more famous more easily.

Les Binet and Peter Field offer empirical evidence to back up this hypothesis. Their analysis of hundreds of IPA effectiveness cases over many years shows that campaigns which are not just enjoyed, but also socially shared, are clearly more effective on virtually all measures:

> ...it is possible to subdivide emotional campaigns into two sub-categories: 'emotional involvement' and 'fame'. Emotional involvement campaigns were those that made people feel differently about the brand in a passive sense, i.e. did not inspire them to the extent that they chose to share their enthusiasm with others. Fame campaigns also made people feel differently about the brand, but did so in a way that inspired them to share their enthusiasm on and offline (buzz and pass along rates are common metrics of this). Thus fame campaigns amplify the positive attributes of emotional involvement in terms of profit growth (2013, p.60).

All this argues that the Rowan Atkinson campaign was especially effective in creating mental availability precisely because it was highly enjoyable as well as distinctive. Audiences watched the ads with high attention levels and even though the best commercials were extensively repeated they showed no signs of wear out. And we know the campaign stimulated considerable word of mouth and media coverage (this was of course long before digital social media enabled people to share ads directly).

But important as fame undoubtedly is, there may be other reasons too why this campaign was so effective. The idea of mental associations, especially emotional ones, may explain how advertising can change not just a brand's mental availability, but the way we feel about it – the kind of relationship we perceive we have with it. This is what I have previously called...

4.   The Relationship model

When I joined Boase Massimi Pollitt in 1974, the agency was only six years old but already had an impressive show reel of ads that were highly popular and entertaining. Many of these campaigns will now be largely forgotten, but British readers may still remember the Smash Martians, the Humphreys which stole Unigate Milk, and the Cresta Bear. Martin Boase, one of our founders, had a saying that 'good advertising doesn't have to be bad', which he would often explain to us in words something like this:

> We believe that if you're going to invite yourself into someone's living room for thirty seconds, you have a duty not to bore them or insult them by shouting at them. On the other hand, if you can make them smile, or show them something interesting or enjoyable – if you're a charming guest – then they may like you a bit better, and then they may be a little more likely to buy your product.

Seen through the lens of this model, one of the most important things about the Barclaycard campaign is how well it did exactly what Martin Boase proposed: it came into people's living rooms, put a smile on their faces, and left them feeling a bit warmer towards the brand. And this was important, because in the absence of advertising like this, the default attitude to credit cards at that time was one of distrust, if not downright hostility. They were seen as organisations that encouraged people to spend money they didn't have, then charged them excessive rates of interest. The Rowan Atkinson campaign encouraged and maintained a very different relationship.

But we can easily see this model as another variation of the mental associations theory. When we use the metaphor of a relationship, it is another way of saying that when ads are associated with feelings of pleasure or of irritation, those feelings become associated with the brand.

You could argue that only matters if you believe that feelings of liking or disliking for the brand influence the likelihood to purchase. And it is true that people do, often, buy brands they don't much like, and brands whose advertising they don't much like.

But other things being equal, it seems very likely that liking the brand and liking the advertising *do* make people more inclined to buy. Daniel Kahneman points out that our System 1 choices are influenced not just by the *availability* heuristic (we choose what comes to mind first) but also by the *affect* heuristic (we choose the ones that we feel good about). The Atkinson campaign therefore may have done more than created specific associations with the brand (e.g. youthfulness, worldwide travel), and more than increased its mental availability: it may have directly increased people's positive affect for the brand, another reason they became more likely to take it out of their wallets. Of course, it is probably pointless to try to tease these different factors too far apart, as they are all mutually reinforcing, all aspects of the overall complex mental associative network which the advertising helped to create for the brand.

The idea that liking and fame (affect and availability) are distinct, and yet also mutually supporting, has been elegantly expressed by Orlando Wood of the System1 research agency:

> There are three key mental shortcuts that help people decide between brands. We call them *Fame*, *Feeling* and *Fluency*. To our fast-thinking, System 1 minds:
>
> + If a brand comes readily to mind, it's a good choice (Fame).
>
> + If a brand feels good, it's a good choice (Feeling).
>
> + If a brand is recognisable, it's a good choice (Fluency).

These rules of thumb are what behavioural scientists call the 'availability heuristic', the 'affect heuristic' and the 'processing fluency heuristic'.

In other words, what I have called the relationship model is entirely consistent with theories of mental associative networks, the importance of affect as well as mental availability, and the trinity of 'fame, feeling, and fluency'. And all together begin to point to strong reasons why apparently trivial or peripheral notions of 'entertainment' can come to assert a powerful influence on choice behaviour on a mass scale.

In *The Anatomy of Humbug* I also proposed a fifth model of how advertising works – by shaping our views of reality. This too can potentially be explained using the idea of mental associative networks. It can also perhaps be applied to the Barclaycard campaign.

5.   The Social Construction, or PR, model.

The pioneers of public relations discovered long ago – much earlier than their colleagues in advertising, and long before Peter Berger and Thomas Luckmann published their seminal work, *The Social Construction of Reality* – that the world we each perceive is not objective and given, but shaped by the stories we are told about it, the language we use about it, and the many ways in which society has evolved shared and predictable habits of dealing with it.

When Edward Bernays, the great pioneer of modern public relations, was briefed in the 1920s by his tobacco clients to change the social taboo against women smoking in public, he engaged a group of young women to light up their Lucky Strikes in front of press photographers at the Fifth Avenue Easter Parade. They then declared that these were their 'torches of freedom', and previously 'unladylike' behaviour was at a stroke reframed as a blow for women's equality.

This kind of 'reframing' is also one of the possible ways in which advertising works. The advertising for Cadbury's Smash which we created at BMP in the early seventies, instead of trying to argue that instant mashed potato was as good as 'the real thing', inverted those values by poking fun at old-fashioned potatoes that had to be laboriously peeled, boiled, and mashed. You can see a similar inversion of values in the Barclaycard campaign. Buying with Barclaycard is always assumed to be the natural, sensible way to do things; the only person who refuses to accept this is the character played by Rowan Atkinson, who is consistently portrayed as stubborn, arrogant, and foolish, and who never learns from the disasters that inevitably make him ridiculous. Rather than presenting the credit card as a status symbol or an innovation, it's absolutely normal for ordinary people like Bough, and *not* using Barclaycard becomes the eccentric and antiquated option.

We can see this, too, as a process of influencing the mental associative networks around Barclaycard. At a literal, pragmatic level it associates the idea of using Barclaycard with the modest, likeable Bough; at a conceptual level, it associates it with everyday normality and sensible, prudent behaviour. 'Hard cash and hard bargaining', like the labour of peeling and boiling potatoes, are conversely linked to obsolescence and a stubborn refusal to change. In the case of Barclaycard, this may not be the single most compelling explanation for the campaign's success, but it's entirely plausible and nothing in it is incompatible with the other patterns of associations already proposed.

Indeed, rather than see these five models as somehow being in competition, each one of them foregrounds a different aspect of the rich, complex, and emotionally loaded mental associative network that the Rowan Atkinson campaign succeeded in creating. This network includes not only subconscious associations, positive feelings, enhanced mental availability and reframed connections and context for the brand, but also the functional benefits spelled out in the 'salesmanship' model. It all fits together, and arguably gains strength from the fact that it seems to work at a number of different levels.

You may be feeling by now that you've had enough of such ponderous intellectual analysis of these commercials. Like having to explain why a joke is funny, it's easy to lose sight of the apparently effortless and 'fluent' way in which we experience the campaign itself. As Wordsworth wrote, 'we murder to dissect', a sentiment endorsed by Bill Bernbach:

> It's like love: the more you analyse it, the more it disappears.

And while psychology may have valuable things to tell us about how advertising works, and therefore act as a much-needed corrective to some of the erroneous assumptions we live by, I believe it doesn't tell us much about how to create such advertising. Science and theory provide valuable covering fire, but they can't do the work of artistry.

So let's now look at the actual process that led to the creation of this campaign. As we shall see, much about this was chaotic, flawed, and mistaken. But there are lessons to be learnt from it, lessons that go beyond anything my typology of models or metaphors might obviously suggest. I will tell the story – as honestly as I can – of what exactly happened, the sequence of events that resulted in this successful campaign becoming a reality.

Chapter Two

From Salesmanship to Showmanship

___

We had won the Barclaycard account after a pitch process that was a model of thoroughness. It was, as usual, a creative pitch, in which each agency had to present the campaign that they would run, if appointed. The Barclaycard people loved our campaign, they seemed to like us as well, and they gave us the business.

However, the campaign that won the pitch for us bore no relation to the ads that eventually appeared.

Barclaycard had a history of celebrity-led advertising – they had originally used the comedian Dudley Moore, followed later by roving reporter Alan Whicker. Despite (or perhaps because of?) these precedents, we told Barclaycard that they didn't need another celebrity. The most talked about ad of the previous twelve months had been British Airways' 'Manhattan', a typically over-the-top big production number from Saatchi and Saatchi. We tried to offer them something a bit like that.

Having endlessly chewed over the client's thorough brief, and conducted our own extensive research, we had emerged with a strategy that was summed up in the end line and proposition – 'Barclaycard: It's all the credit cards you'll ever need'.

To dramatise this thought, our blockbuster commercial opened on an aerial shot of a great city. We would zoom in to see hordes of people excitedly running up the stairs of the skyscrapers to the rooftops. There they would begin cutting all their other credit cards into bits and throwing them into the air. We would see people below at cafe tables mystified as fragments of credit card fell into their cappuccinos. Dramatic music would build to a climax as a voice-over listed the new product benefits of Barclaycard, leading to the conclusion: 'We think it's all the credit cards you'll ever need.'

The client loved it. So did we. But as we started working on it (with several months still before the relaunch date), problems began to emerge.

The first was the consumer research, conducted by an independent research company. They reported that respondents in focus groups were variously puzzled, sceptical, and generally underwhelmed. However, they were anxious not to seem too negative towards our great pitch-winning script, and assured us it could be got right with a bit of tweaking. (Many agencies are heartily sceptical of this or any kind of pre-testing research, but we weren't – we used it all the time and knew that it often led to better work. So we went along with it.)

The second was the budget. We always knew this was an expensive film, but the initial quotes for production were astronomical. We started to look at how the idea could be scaled down a bit.

The third was the ITV copy clearance committee, who pointed out that any identification of competitors' cards would be forbidden, and that throwing rubbish off buildings could not be allowed because it would encourage litter.

Six months passed, with endless rewrites, another round of research, renegotiations with producers and with the copy clearance committee. By the third round of research we had an animatic featuring a solitary man in a mackintosh, standing on a fire escape, cutting up a couple of credit cards and putting them into a paper bag. Needless to say, it bombed in research worse than ever.

It was now getting desperately close to the relaunch date, so we started again from scratch. Some scripts were written which dramatised what could go wrong if you went away on holiday without a Barclaycard. Research was hurriedly set up, and as the deadline was too tight to use the same research company, I was allowed to moderate these groups myself. At the eleventh hour, mild panic set in and we decided we needed another option, just in case the new scripts flopped too. One of the creative teams had an idea involving Rowan Atkinson. Even this was nothing like the finished films. It was based on the idea of Atkinson taking over Whicker's roving reporter role, initially even wearing a false moustache, but getting it all wrong.

When I took the two sets of animatics out to the great British public, it turned out they didn't think much of either. The first campaign was voted gloomy and boring and was actively disliked. The Atkinson campaign simply wasn't very funny – mildly embarrassing, in fact.

It didn't take very long to find all that out, so in some desperation I asked the respondents what they thought we should do next. And the best answers that came back were all along the same lines: 'You should use Rowan Atkinson anyway, because he's usually funny whatever he does.'

Somehow – using account management skills of the highest order – we managed to persuade our client that we now had a clear way forward. Fortunately, Atkinson was willing to do advertising, only not as himself. He had his own idea for a new character, a secret agent : he gave us this overall concept, and our creative teams began to write scripts around it. John Lloyd, Atkinson's trusted producer on other ventures, was engaged to direct the films.

There was no time for further research. We simply had to trust the people and the direction we now had. Atkinson and Lloyd and the agency team worked endlessly long days on the shoots, rewriting the scripts as they went. The results, at best, were little masterpieces of comic film-making.

We held our collective breath as the first films went on air. With no time for pre-testing, we very quickly did in-market quantitative research to monitor the public reaction. Not only were the films voted highly enjoyable, but it was clear they also communicated the product benefits – still the thing the client was most worried about. Within a month or so, association of Rowan Atkinson with Barclaycard exceeded the already high figure for Alan Whicker. The campaign ran for several years, with results as already described, and it only stopped when eventually Rowan Atkinson decided he didn't want to do any more.

*

If you've worked in advertising, you may have experienced a sneaking recognition that a lot of campaigns emerge from a process something like this – messy, chaotic, and with more than a dash of what seems like pure fluke. Jeremy Bullmore, reviewing an earlier version of this story, took this view:

> It's possible that the only honest case-study in the history of marketing is the Barclaycard case written by Paul Feldwick... it describes in hilarious detail just how luck, agency obduracy and a collision of events entirely fortuitously led to an award-winning campaign of great commercial effectiveness.

Jeremy observes that published case histories about ad campaigns virtually never tell what really happened (if you read the version of the Barclaycard story that was published in the IPA Effectiveness Case Studies you will be given the impression of a seamless progress from strategy to execution, with none of the blind alleys or crises that actually occurred), and he compares this situation to a famous essay by the Nobel-winning scientist, Sir Peter Medawar, which makes exactly the same point about scientific papers. While papers accepted for publication in scientific journals always seem to describe a logical and elegant process from thought to experiment to conclusion, in reality the process of scientific discovery is one of muddle, stuckness, and (when you're lucky) some kind of breakthrough.

It seems that in both scientific discovery and advertising creation, the honest stories are never told – they are generally seen as embarrassing, as evidence of some kind of failure. But they really need to be told, because otherwise nothing can be learnt from these experiences. It would be a mistake simply to sum up the Barclaycard story as another example of 'we wasted our time getting it all wrong for six months, and then pulled a rabbit out of the hat at the last minute'. That is the sort of story that advertising people like to tell each other in the pub in a self-deprecating way, and of course there is a kind of truth in it. But there is not much to be *learnt* from telling the story that way; nor, with great respect to Jeremy Bullmore, is it enough to conclude that eventual success was 'entirely fortuitous'. We could instead reflect on such questions as: why did it take us so long to find the right direction? what, maybe, did we actually do right that might have helped us get there in the end? And what could we try doing differently in future?

One thing I notice now is how hard we had all worked to make the process neat, organised, controlled. We did everything 'by the book'. There was no shortage of time, due diligence, or intelligence. The client brief could not have been more thorough. The agency interviewed everyone in the client organisation. The pitch process was rigorous, fair, numerically scored. The best researchers were hired. We all seemed to get on together terribly well. What could possibly go wrong?

Yet I suspect that in terms of directly fulfilling the task, all this elaborate ritual achieved little, beyond containing the anxiety that is inevitable in such a highly charged situation. I also suspect that it was precisely our desire to avoid overt conflict or confusion that got in the way of learning or discovery happening earlier than it did. The same quality of 'groupthink' that was observed among policy makers in the Vietnam War made it impossible for anyone, in the client or agency teams, to suggest that our Great Pitch Winning Idea might be fundamentally flawed; and the researchers too played along with this by refusing to put the campaign out of its misery six months sooner. With hindsight, there were plenty of signals that should have made us challenge our thinking, but we colluded in ignoring them.

On the other hand, given that such classic mistakes had been made and much time lost, everyone on the team deserves credit for their adaptability and trust when the failure of the initial plan could no longer be ignored. The stakes were genuinely high for the business, and it would have been very easy at that point for the energy released by the crisis to be dissipated in mutual recriminations, and redoubled efforts at analysis and control – which would, almost certainly, have included the firing of the agency. Anyone could have blocked the campaign that finally emerged – the marketing director, the CEO, the agency planners, the researcher, the creative department. That none of them did is an achievement for which everyone deserves respect. It also suggests to me that in this case, the amount of time we had all spent together as a team, especially in face to face contact, had built a sufficiently high level of trust, so in that sense the elaborate rituals of the pitch were perhaps valuable.

One thing we could learn from this story, then, is that any creative process is likely to involve iterations of trial and error, which almost inevitably create high levels of anxiety, confusion, and conflict. Most organisations act on the basis of avoiding the anxiety, either by keeping things neat and orderly, or by destructive conflict and blame – fight or flight reactions, which prevent the group from confronting the anxiety and working through it. One way of reading the Barclaycard case is to notice how we spent a long time avoiding anxiety and confusion, and then – only when we were forced to – did we finally succeed in confronting it and working through it. This is probably a common pattern, and not only in advertising, and perhaps we could learn from it that confronting the anxiety earlier may be possible and desirable.

One dimension of learning from experience is to reflect on what was done, and how it could have been done differently. But another dimension is to make explicit what shared assumptions and beliefs underpinned that behaviour. Such assumptions and beliefs are often entirely unconscious and so taken for granted that, at the time, no-one even thinks to put them into words, let alone challenge them. So we can also re-interpret this case now through the lens of the shared assumptions we were making about how we expected the advertising to work.

To the best of my recollection, we never discussed this at the time, and we certainly lacked the language of 'implicit models' which I developed much later in *The Anatomy of Humbug* and which I reviewed in the previous chapter. Nevertheless, the point about implicit models is that they control our behaviour precisely because we are unaware of them – that's why they're called 'implicit', and, because we cannot argue against them, they become such powerful constraints.

So in the belief that our 'implicit models' formed an unrecognised but powerful influence on our shared patterns of behaviour, I shall try to reconstruct what they might have been.

It seems clear to me now that from the beginning we tacitly defaulted – as usually happens – to a version of the Salesmanship model, in which the transmission of the *proposition* ('it's all the credit cards you'll ever need') and the *reasons why* (the various product innovations) were our guiding principles. The pitch campaign was based on dramatising the *proposition*, a verbal message that was meant to summarise why our product was better. This line, 'all the credit cards you'll ever need' subsequently, of course, vanished without trace! The 'reasons why' were not dramatised in the original ad, merely mentioned in the voice over. By attempting to reduce a potentially complex story to one single proposition we were following a strongly held piece of advertising orthodoxy, which can be traced back to Rosser Reeves, that 'people only remember one thing from an advert'. The dramatic film which we proposed was merely a device to get attention, and to make the 'single-minded proposition' memorable.

Our pitch presentation, using this implicit model, showed a clear linear progression – from analysis of the situation, to a statement of strategy which in turn became our proposition, which then structured the advert itself. This kind of step by step thinking often wins pitches: everything can be justified on the basis of what's gone before, nothing appears too arbitrary or surprising. And this also largely explains the continued dominance of the Salesmanship model in advertising practice: it lends itself ideally to such a process of apparently logical development.

The second campaign, which attempted to dramatise the new card benefits (the 'reasons why') by showing what could happen if you didn't have them, was still working within the framework of the Salesmanship model. But the original Rowan Atkinson campaign which was tested alongside it was doing something rather different. By heavily referencing the previous campaign with Alan Whicker, it was making use of an established distinctive asset, instantly recognisable and uniquely associated with the brand. This campaign was based less on a Salesmanship model and much more on a Salience model, with particular emphasis on the protection of an existing distinctive asset or fluent device. We and the client had all agreed that it was time to drop Whicker, yet now we were intuitively reverting towards finding a 'safe' way to replace him with Atkinson as a distinctive asset for the brand.

As I explained earlier, neither of these second-wave campaigns researched well as animatics. The first was found dull, gloomy, and confusing – it offered people nothing of enjoyment or of interest and, as so often, they disliked merely being lectured to. The Atkinson-as-Whicker campaign was marginally more interesting, but it depended for its effect entirely on humour – and, as such, it simply wasn't funny enough.

What our respondents could see however, perhaps more clearly than we could at first, was that it brought a new, unexpected, and stimulating element into the situation – Rowan Atkinson, who at that time, had recently become extremely famous and popular. The proposal to 'use Rowan Atkinson because he's funny' was therefore not as trivial as it sounds. Unlike all the logical, step by step thinking that we had previously relied on, we were now clearly looking at something illogical, arbitrary, and exciting. Atkinson's own idea to appear as a new character, the comic secret agent Richard Latham, took this a major step further. Something had now been created, something that had not been there before – something that was not logically predictable from our analysis or strategy or proposition.

And from this point on, as I remember the process, we weren't just making ads – we were putting on a show. From the crisis onward, we were less driven by the demands of Salesmanship and increasingly following the rules of Showmanship. The focus of all our collective actions moved away from strategies, propositions, and reasons why, to embrace a radically different set of implied goals: How can we make this *famous*? How can we make it *funny*? How can we create a piece of spectacularly good *entertainment*? Because that's what absorbed everyone's time and effort from that moment on.

So we ended up tacitly buying into a sixth model, consistent with yet qualitatively different from the other five, and one which we'd actually been resisting all along in our quest for a controlled, logical process and a campaign that communicated a selling proposition. This is what, in *The Anatomy of Humbug*, I called

6.   The Showmanship, or Humbug, Model.

You could say that the Showmanship model merely builds on ideas that I have already presented: it recognises the importance of fame, the use of distinctive assets, the affect heuristic, the creation of a positive relationship with the audience. Yet it also represents a completely different mindset for creating brand-building advertising, one in which entertainment becomes central rather than just a technique or a means to an end. To get a sense of this mindset we need to go back to many years before Lasker, Kennedy, Hopkins and Reeves indoctrinated us advertising practitioners in the framework of salesmanship, benefits, and the reason why – back to the early nineteenth century, and the character and career of the 'greatest showman', Phineas T. Barnum.

Barnum has long been ignored or even disowned by the advertising business, yet his techniques in many ways lay the foundation of both modern popular culture and modern publicity – two things which, after all, have always been utterly dependent on each other. This is both glaringly obvious, and yet remarkably little talked about in advertising and marketing circles. The high and serious science of selling dominates the professional discourse, while the vulgarity and ostensible triviality of entertainment is at best tacitly tolerated, at worst contemptuously rejected.

It was Barnum who ironically reclaimed the word 'humbug' – originally meaning a fraud or deceit. He boasted of himself as 'the Prince of Humbugs', and wrote a popular book called *Great Humbugs of the World*. In this he explained why humbug was not the same as fraud:

> 'Humbug' consists in putting on glittering appearances – outside show – novel expedients, by which to suddenly arrest public attention, and attract the public eye and ear… An honest man who thus arrests public attention will be called a 'humbug', but he is not a swindler or an impostor (Cook, p.95).

In a time when we're coming to revalue and understand the nature of 'mental availability', and the complexities of creating fame through a combination of interest, pleasure, and distinctive assets, it seems to me it's also time to revalue Barnum, who had already, long ago, got to a very similar place. More than anyone else, Barnum deserves credit for demonstrating how fame could be created on an industrial scale, and for purely commercial purposes. The content of what he did was not in itself new – novelty, entertainment, the curious or bizarre – his innovations were in the way he exploited advances in communications to reach mass audiences across wide geographies, and in his ability to create identities which were unique and ownable. There were many elephants, but only one Jumbo; many singers, but only one Jenny Lind; many dwarf entertainers, but only one Colonel Tom Thumb. Such 'celebrities' closely anticipate the world of brands, but above all the greatest 'brand' that Barnum created was Barnum himself; he did this deliberately and with immense energy, fully aware of its commercial value, so that towards the end of his life he could claim, probably correctly, that he was the most famous person in the world.

Barnum is historically significant, not just because he was a successful entertainer – though this was an integral part of what he did – but because he set the template for how successful celebrities, and successful brands, are created. While today's marketers and agencies tie themselves in knots over the many layers of convoluted theory that have accrued around the topic of brands – *positioning, values, image, essence, purpose,* and so on – I fear they tend to overlook a much simpler construct for building brands, the construct of *fame.* Advertising is by no means the only way to create fame, but it is one possible route: and arguably, creating fame is the most important role of advertising.

This, put in simple language, is very close to the Ehrenberg-Bass formula for how brands grow – a combination of maximising physical and mental availability. So you could argue that what I have called the Showmanship model is fundamentally the Fame or Salience model under another name, perhaps with a mixture of the Relationship model and even hints of a few others thrown in.

But using words like Showmanship, or, even more, Humbug, creates a very different feeling from the detached language of 'mental availability'. It reminds us that there is no simple recipe for creating fame, nor can it be done in a purely calculating and clinical way; it needs the energy, imagination, risk taking, and shameless braggadocio that street entertainers and charlatans have relied on in all ages. Humbug is not afraid of vulgarity, childishness, the sensational or the erotic, though it can equally affect high principles when it chooses to; its archetype is the Trickster, and its spirit is the spirit of carnival. And the advertising business ever since its earliest days has struggled to deny its connection with this carnival world of popular culture, while at the same time tacitly depending on it for its effects.

Within the terms of this model, the Barclaycard campaign is not just incidentally entertaining. It is fundamentally a *show* designed to attract and keep its audience, with high craft skills and a top ranking star, as a means to creating mental availability and liking uniquely for Barclaycard.

*

We resisted and fought against the Showmanship model most of the way, but were bumped into it, in the end, by two things. One was the sheer crisis created by an inflexible deadline: doing nothing was not an option, and there was no possibility of buying extra time, so we (fortunately) chose to make the best of what was available. The other was the positive energy generated by being presented with something actual and specific, something that we could find exciting and believe in. We were no longer looking at a blank sheet of paper and vainly trying to fill it with logical ideas: we now had our stars, we had our director, we had our characters and basic scenario. We were no longer working from an intellectual, verbal abstraction, but with actual human characters and situations. We were no longer limiting ourselves to cautious, step by step thinking, as we had already been bounced into making the leap to something arbitrary, distinctive, and appealing. We knew that we had to make a success of it, and we now believed we could. And so we did.

But why did we need to be 'bumped into it' at all? Why were we so long seduced by the rational, message-transmission, Salesmanship model – even for a brand whose history of using celebrities and entertainment was patently obvious? I do not think this was a merely local or temporary oversight on our part. It is better understood as symptomatic of a deep confusion in advertising thinking which goes very far back – certainly more than a century. If we are to address the difficulties we currently face in a rapidly changing world of new technology and new media, we may need to go back before we can go forward, in order to understand the roots of these entrenched assumptions.

Chapter Three
Who Framed Sunny Jim?

In 1901 Edward Ellsworth, the owner of several cereal mills in the mid-West, decided that if he were to make a success of his new breakfast cereal, Force, he needed to advertise.

The market for pre-packed cereals was about to take off. A few years earlier Henry Parsons Crowell had transformed the fortunes of Quaker Oats by a combination of efficient mass production, a distinctive trademark, colourful individual packaging and heavy media advertising. C.W. Post and the Kellogg brothers were promoting the health benefits of a lighter, cereal breakfast, but the only cold cereal yet marketed on a wide scale was Post's Grape Nuts : Shredded Wheat, Corn Flakes and Post Toasties were all yet to become popular brands. Force, a wheat flake that needed no cooking, was looking at a major opportunity.

On a trip to New York, Ellsworth's advertising manager commissioned a young woman called Minnie Maud Hanff to write some ads. At the age of twenty-three, Hanff already had several years' experience writing rhymes and children's articles for New York newspapers. She took a similarly light-hearted approach to Force, writing rhymes about a grumpy man whose life was changed by eating the cereal:

> Jim Dumps was a most unfriendly man
> Who lived his life on the hermit plan;
> In his gloomy way he'd gone through life,
> And made the most of woe and strife;
> Till Force one day was served to him –
> Since then they've called him 'Sunny Jim'.

Hanff's friend Dorothy Ficken, who was still in high school at that time, drew Sunny Jim as a comical cartoon character in an odd eighteenth-century costume, with top hat and waistcoat; he sported a walking cane and a distinctive pigtail. Interviewed for the trade magazine *Printers' Ink* in 1902, Hanff revealed that Ellsworth had only bought the campaign after seeing Ficken's illustrations. She also explained why she'd approached the advertising brief as she did:

> Goodness gracious! A breakfast cereal isn't all life, is it? People are not going to
> take it nearly as seriously as the advertiser wants them to. They see the ad for
> a single minute, and I thought it better to give them a minute's entertainment.

The media placement was handled directly by the Force company, without an agency. The campaign became a rapid success. The public started sending in their own Sunny Jim rhymes by the hundred. A seaside cave in La Jolla, California was named 'Sunny Jim', as its opening resembled his pigtailed silhouette. Songs and comedies were written about him. *Printers' Ink* remarked that

> No current novel or play is so universally popular. He is as well known as
> President Roosevelt or J. Pierpont Morgan.

And yet – Sunny Jim would become notorious in advertising history as an example of a campaign that achieved popular fame, but failed to sell the product. It would be cited even generations later by proponents of the 'hard sell', as proof that mere entertainment is not enough. In 1908, the advertising manager of the Western Clock Manufacturing Company wrote in a memo to his directors:

> I would not recommend any so-called 'clever' advertising or humorous copy...
> for instance like the Sunny Jim campaign...

In 1914 G.H.E. Hawkins wrote, in an influential book on newspaper advertising:

> He was a national character while he existed, but the trouble was there wasn't
> enough connection between 'Sunny Jim' and the product.

And at the time of Minnie Hanff's death, in 1943, *Printers' Ink* wondered:

> Couldn't it be said that optimistic advertisers, who find their advertising getting
> public attention but not sales, have a 'Sunny Jim' on their hands?

Even Stephen Fox, who tells this part of the Sunny Jim story in his classic 1984 history of American advertising, *The Mirror Makers*, concurs with this verdict, reflecting sadly that 'Great popularity, it seemed, did not necessarily translate into sales'.

*

However, it has now been shown that this damning judgement on the effectiveness of the Sunny Jim campaign is completely unjustified. And the real story, as unearthed and published in a 2001 paper by Eileen Margerum of Salem State University, tells us some fascinating and important things both about brands, and about the culture of the ad business.

So what happened after the initial launch of Sunny Jim?

Edward Ellsworth owned another cereal brand called H-O. Even as the Force campaign was attracting initial success, he invited the newly founded New York advertising agency of Calkins and Holden to his head office in Buffalo, to pitch for the H-O business.

Earnest Elmo Calkins's life was shaped by a bout of measles at the age of six which left him profoundly deaf. After college he found a job writing copy for the Charles Austin Bates agency in New York, where he met Ralph Holden, whose outgoing character was complementary to his more introverted partner. Calkins would become an important figure in the history of advertising. In many ways the diametric opposite of his contemporary and rival, Claude Hopkins, Calkins valued the importance of design and art, and of copy that would entertain as well as inform. About this time he produced a celebrated campaign, also in rhyme, for the Lackawanna Railroad, inventing a character called Phoebe Snow whose clothes always remained 'spotless white/Upon the road of anthracite'.

Calkins and Holden were effective promoters of their own agency too, and on their visit to Ellsworth (presumably via the Lackawanna Railroad, which ran from Hoboken to Buffalo) they persuaded him that they should take over the Force account along with H-O, arguing no doubt that the growing brand now deserved the attention of real professionals. As soon as their agency was appointed, Calkins made major changes to the Sunny Jim campaign, in a way that will seem familiar to anyone in the ad business. He kept the character's name, but that was about all. Out went the rhymes and Dorothy Ficken's innocent drawings. In their place, a new style of illustration reinvented Sunny Jim as a rather weird and sinister figure, while solid blocks of prose lectured the reader on a mixture of nutrition and 'positive thinking', always ending with the words 'Be Sunny!'

Yet, by this time, the original campaign had been running for some two or three years, and its effects on sales had, as far as we can tell, been spectacular: according to an article in *Canadian Grocer*, the output of one mill at the start of the campaign had already increased to the output of four, together producing 360,000 packages each day. I have no idea what Force retailed at, but guessing at a conservative 5 cents a package, the price of a loaf of bread, this represents a substantial annual turnover of $6.5 million.

The exact details of what happened next are obscure, but it seems that Calkins's revised version of Sunny Jim failed to maintain the momentum of the business, the agency was fired (Calkins later claiming that Ellsworth failed to pay them what he owed), and the campaign discontinued. Soon afterwards, Ellsworth mismanaged other aspects of the business, and his creditors, mainly banks, took control. The Force brand was then sold to the Hecker Company, and subsequently changed hands several times.

With the change of campaign, and subsequent loss of support for the brand, it seems that the sales growth of Force stalled – just at the time when Kellogg's was beginning to advertise Corn Flakes nationally for the first time, and C. W. Post was launching Post Toasties. It is easy to see how the eclipse of Force in the US contributed to the belief that Sunny Jim had failed in generating sales, despite his popularity. But there are other reasons too why Sunny Jim took the blame for the decline in Force's fortunes.

Right from the outset the Sunny Jim campaign had been controversial. In the 1902 *Printers' Ink* article in which Minnie Hanff was interviewed, the author, James Collins, described the industry reaction to the campaign:

> … there was an instant chorus of disappointment from those who 'knew' good publicity when they saw it. Many of the critics suffered pangs of real grief that money should be wasted in so wanton a way, and the advertising craft in general seemed confident that the Force folks had finally reached the utmost bounds of vapidity: 'Punk!' said some. 'Rotten!' said others. 'Good Lord!' said still others… when a firm is spending hundreds of thousands of dollars for space it would seem the plainest business sense to pay a decent salary to a man who could write good copy.

There is a clue in that last sentence. It wasn't just the use of rhyme and child-like drawings: campaigns like Sapolio soap and the Lackawanna Railroad had already done similar things. Eileen Margerum concludes that

> The real cause of their dislike is rooted much deeper: the advertising craft was afraid of what the real success of the Sunny Jim campaign represented. Advertising was still struggling to be taken seriously as a reputable and necessary part of American business culture. This campaign challenged all the claims to special expertise being made by Calkins and his advertising brethren. It was written and drawn by two 'girls', as they are described in the [Collins] article… In addition, members of the public wrote their own jingles, as if they, too, could write ad copy.

> A third reason… was that the campaign was being run by amateurs: Ellsworth and his staff in Buffalo were deciding when and where to place the ads. If the

Sunny Jim campaign were acknowledged as a success, it would cast doubt on the new foundations of the American advertising industry. Ultimately the answer was simple: declare the campaign a failure, despite all the evidence to the contrary.

For Calkins himself, the whole experience rankled throughout his long life. He later declared he had hated the original campaign right from the start. He was committed to the idea that advertising should be professionalised, and thought only the best sort of Ivy League graduates should be employed as copywriters – certainly not a couple of 'girls'. In his many books and writings on advertising he repeatedly distanced himself from the stigma that had attached to Sunny Jim, and in the process did all he could to reinforce the myth of its ineffectiveness:

> The advertising absolutely sold Sunny Jim to the public, but it did not sell Force. Humor, you see, is a very good servant but a bad master.

Despite everything, Sunny Jim and Force lived to fight another day – in the United Kingdom. The brand was launched there in 1903, with the same Hanff-Ficken creative work. It seems that on this side of the Atlantic the brand had a similar initial success, but was then allowed to continue with it. Sunny Jim evolved into an even more engaging character, and the jingles were replaced by the simple rhyme:

> High o'er the fence leaps Sunny Jim
> Force is the food that raises him.

By the 1920s, Sunny Jim dolls had become widely popular as a way of merchandising the brand; my mother, who was a little girl at the time, vividly remembered having one, and could still recite 'High o'er the fence...' many decades later. Following from this success, there was a short-lived attempt to reintroduce Sunny Jim to the USA in the 1930s, but again, it was not followed through. In the UK, however, the character and the brand continued to flourish, with a wide variety of promotional character merchandise from yo-yos to gramophone records, and advertising on Radio Luxembourg. The last version of the Sunny Jim doll appeared in 1976 and sold well into the next decade (again, I remember my mother buying one for my younger sister, a tribute to how the character had lodged in her affections). The brand is still sold widely in the UK, though its market share today is not large; it is now owned by Nestlé.

It is true to say that Force never lived up to the potential which its publicity created, and in that sense it demonstrates that 'fame alone' is not enough: fame needs to be maintained over time, to be supported by a good enough product and good distribution, and to be part of a sustainable business model. But the weakness of Force lay not with its advertising executions or its distinctive asset, Sunny Jim – it was just about everything else that restricted its growth below what it might have been.

Some may see this episode as nothing more than a footnote in advertising's distant past. Others will, and rightly, take it as a small example of the way women, in so many different fields, have been systematically written out of history. Though this is an important aspect of the story, it is also about more than this. The story of Sunny Jim is symptomatic of a crisis in the self-image of the advertising business which began around the first decade of the twentieth century (the so-called 'Progressive Age' of American business), and is arguably still with us today.

From about 1900 on, as advertising became big business, agencies aspired to a kind of respectability and professional status that might ultimately rank them alongside lawyers or doctors – and conversely, sever their historical links with the fraudulent claims of patent medicines and the vulgar entertainments of the medicine shows. Advertising Clubs were formed, and codes of ethics created, including what became known as the 'truth in advertising movement'.

The quest for professionalism was understandable, some aspects of it necessary and even admirable: a lot in advertising's past had its disgraceful side. But along with the genuinely shoddy and dishonest practices, the new technical/ rational world of advertising also attempted to disown and deny qualities that have always been central to successful selling and brand creation – qualities of playfulness, subversion, popular appeal, ambiguity, the pleasures of the childish and the illogical, the carnival world of satire, eroticism, talking animals and general nonsense – everything that the emerging professional/managerial culture despised and rejected.

As the cultural historian Jackson Lears expressed it in his book, *Fables of Abundance*,

> Advertising executives and copywriters were confronted with a fundamental conflict. The professional-managerial worldview put a scientific gloss on Protestant plain speech: in epistemological matters it created a vast apparatus for disproving and verifying universalist truth-claims... Yet the ad makers themselves came out of a carnivalesque tradition that subverted unified meaning and promoted the pursuit of success through persuasion, theatricality, and outright trickery (p.212).

It is no coincidence that two other significant events in advertising history happened around the time of the original Sunny Jim campaign. It was in 1903 that the freelance copywriter John E. Kennedy blagged his way into the Chicago office of Albert Lasker, the young managing director of the Lord and Thomas ad agency, to tell him his new definition of advertising as 'salesmanship in print' – a formula which established Lord and Thomas as the home of 'reason why' advertising, and the biggest agency in the world. In telling this story at length in *The Anatomy of Humbug*, I suggested this was a symbolic start point for the subsequent domination of advertising thinking by models of rational persuasion and message transmission, what I have called the 'Salesmanship' model of advertising. About the same time, Walter Dill Scott at Northwestern University in nearby Evanston was publishing the first version of his book, *The Psychology of Advertising*, in which he offered a very different theory – that advertising principally worked by creating subconscious associations or 'suggestions'. As we've seen, this alternative model would later become fashionable in the 'motivation research' movement of the 1950's; but it was ultimately always fated to be eclipsed by the simple plausibility and 'plain speech' of the salesmanship model. These two different events each signify an aspect of the advertising business's desire to 'professionalise' itself – one through adopting the discourse of rationality and business, the other through the discourse of science.

Both implicitly but firmly moved away from advertising's earlier incarnation as showmanship. Some objected, like one critic who wrote in *Printers' Ink* that good advertising depended on 'good judgment, good taste, good ideas, and a whole lot of other good things that [could not] be dissected or analysed by the college professor' (Schultze). Yet the appeal of 'science', rules, and rationality was stronger.

One powerful advocate for the professional status of advertising was Earnest Elmo Calkins. He argued for advertising as a beneficial social force:

> The effect of such endeavours is beneficial to all – to the public, to the advertiser, to his employee, to the shopkeepers who distribute his goods, and to the conduct of all business (Lears, p.204).

And he envisaged an 'advertising college' that would 'teach advertising as other professional schools now teach other professions', in a rigorous three year, full time course (not the thirty day correspondence courses that were now springing up).

> Such a school will make its appeal to the public in the same dignified, conservative way that a good law or medicine school makes its appeal (Schultze).

Clearly there was to be no room in the future advertising profession for untrained 'girls' like Minnie Maud Hanff. Nor, indeed, for the shade of Phineas T. Barnum. *Printers' Ink* refused to celebrate the centenary of the great showman's birth, in 1910, saying it would be like doctors honouring quack medicine: Barnum, they said, had

> played upon a streak of American character which is rapidly declining – the streak of bizarre appetite for the abnormal, the admiration for trickery and the fascination of the horrible (Lears, p.214).

This tension between the desire to be a technical-rational profession, and the subversive, playful spirit of what I like to call humbug, the unacknowledged legacy of Barnum, has bedevilled the advertising business ever since the creation of Sunny Jim. It has played out in complicated and subtle ways. On the face of it, the professional discourse has always been the dominant one. It has shaped the language and processes and the espoused theories of how advertising works, in ways most likely to appeal to and fit in with the rational, organised culture of business. Hence, the various versions of what I have called the 'salesmanship' theories of advertising – rational persuasion, communication of facts, conscious attention, message transmission and message recall – have persistently shaped (and been reinforced by) processes for briefing, decision making, and research.

Yet despite all this, the connections between advertising and the world of entertainment have remained both ubiquitous and obvious. Advertising in all ages has routinely used all the devices and tropes of popular culture: music, song, dance, humour, drama, sex appeal. It makes extensive use of celebrities of all kinds, it borrows fictional characters from the worlds of film, TV, and cartoon, and it creates its own: human, quasi-human, animals anthropomorphic or otherwise – the Jolly Green Giant, the Pillsbury Doughboy, Tony the Tiger, the Dulux dog.

It also exists almost entirely within a context created by popular culture, the world of mass media, a context with which it has sometimes blended and at other times remained distinct. At certain periods of history, there were no clear barriers between programmes or editorial and advertising, and part of the ad agencies' role was the creation of client-sponsored programming. Yet even then, it seems, there were strong factions within the agencies who didn't want to be tarnished by being part of the entertainment business, like the Copy Chief of the fictional Kimberley and Maag agency in Frederic Wakeman's 1946 novel, *The Hucksters*:

> 'Godammit', he said, 'we're ad makers not talent agents. These people in Detroit need good *salesmanship* first and that's the basis on which we should talk to them. I think Kimberley and Maag should be sold on its merits *as a business firm*, not as a peddler of radio comedians. It's a cheap business and I don't want it.' (p.87, *emphasis added*)

Both the connection and the distance between advertising and entertainment are symbolically dramatised in *The Hucksters* as the main character, Vic Norman, makes the three day train journey between New York City and Los Angeles. (Flying was technically possible in 1946, but unavailable for civilians so soon after the war.) Being an adman, Norman will travel only on the fastest and smartest trains – the Twentieth Century Limited to Chicago, and then the Super Chief from Chicago to L.A. – despite the fact that berths on them can only be obtained through bribery and pulling a lot of strings. The differences between the 'business' world of New York and the 'showbusiness' world of L.A. are often remarked on, as when the executives board the Super Chief in Chicago:

> The men still wore their business suits and loud ties; but Vic knew that once on the train they would change into the Hollywood uniform: a sports jacket or shirt, no tie, slacks and moccasins (p.108).

The distance, actual and cultural, between East Coast and West Coast continues to be a powerful metaphor for the gap between 'business' and entertainment – despite the obvious irony that entertainment is just as much a business as anything else. But historically, advertising agencies have striven to identify themselves with the sharp-suited professionals of the East Coast, rather than the vulgar world of 'showbiz'. Through the ages, the admen who have most influenced the culture of the business have thundered against any kind of entertainment in advertising with the rage of Puritan preachers. Claude Hopkins wrote:

> Don't treat your subject lightly. Don't lessen respect for yourself or your article by any attempt at frivolity. People do not patronize a clown...

He was echoed decades later by David Ogilvy:

> Don't *sing* your selling message. Selling is a serious business.

Even Bill Bernbach, the leader of the so-called 'creative revolution' of the 1960s, repeatedly emphasised that the kind of 'creativity' practised in ad agencies should never be confused with mere entertainment: it was always to be harnessed to the serious task of conveying a sales message:

> Merely to let your imagination run riot, to dream unrelated dreams, to indulge in graphic acrobatics and verbal gymnastics is NOT being creative. The creative person has harnessed his imagination. He has disciplined it so that every thought, every idea, every word he puts down, every line he draws, every light and shadow in every photograph he takes, makes more vivid, more *believable*, more *persuasive* the *original theme or product advantage he has decided he must convey* (emphasis added).

So from an early date, the advertising 'profession' – as it liked to think of itself – has been wary and contemptuous of any connection with the world of entertainment. But, as we shall see, they have only been able to maintain this stance by closing their eyes to a great deal of the blindingly obvious.

Because despite the eminence of the authorities solemnly warning marketers that 'selling is a serious business' and 'people do not patronize a clown', such generalisations are not true, and never were.

Chapter Four

Because singers sell soap, Mr Norman

In Act 4 of *The Winter's Tale*, we are at a house in the country when a servant enters to announce a visitor:

> O master! If you did but hear the pedlar at the door, you would never dance again after a tabor and pipe; no, the bagpipe could not move you: he sings several tunes, faster than you'll tell money: he utters them as he had eaten ballads, and all men's ears grow to his tunes...

The servant's excitement reminds us what a novelty it would have been, in any rural society before the invention of recording or broadcasting, for a talented performer to arrive with new songs. But this visitor isn't just an entertainer – he's a pedlar, and he's here to sell things. The servant continues:

> He hath ribbons of all the colours i'th'rainbow; points, more than all the lawyers in Bohemia can learnedly handle, though they come to him by th' gross; inkles, caddises, cambrics, lawns: why, he sings 'em over, as they were

gods or goddesses; you would think a smock were a she-angel, he so chants to the sleeve-hand, and the work about the square on't.

The pedlar himself soon enters and sings a song about his wares, which ends

Come buy of me, come: come buy, come buy,
Buy lads, or else your lasses cry: Come, buy!

The arrival of this travelling salesman and entertainer (who also turns out to be a bit of a rogue) is a fiction in a play, but it's presumably based on a common reality that would have been familiar to Shakespeare and his audience. And in the image of this 'pedlar at the door' I think we can see a point of origin for all modern advertising – one that we too often ignore.

Why does the pedlar sing? It seems to be important not just that he sings, but that he has to sing well – well enough to create genuine excitement and enthusiasm in the servant who hears him. It isn't just about getting noticed, though that may be the start of it; it's perhaps more about making himself acceptable, so that people will invite him in, rather than chase him away. But I think it's more than that too. The songs are there to put the audience in a good mood, and also to make the goods for sale appear more attractive and desirable. At every step, the quality of the entertainment is designed to increase the chance of a sale.

Chantal Thomas, a French sociologist, co-wrote a fascinating essay about advertising with Claude Bonnange (the B of TBWA) which stresses the origins of advertising in carnival, travelling shows and street hawkers:

We want above all, throughout this brief historical overview, to draw attention to an aspect of advertising which is too often forgotten today: a certain openness, an innocence which we find in the earliest forms of advertising. It comes just as much from a liking for spectacle, for playing with words, for putting on a performance, as it does from a desire to sell. These two things are intimately bound together: the actual sale is only one element in the acting out of a shared event, which is infinitely richer than the simple two-way relationship of seller and buyer...

… and people buy, not because they have a need for something (even an illusory one), but as an act of good-humoured participation in the fleeting moment of entertainment which the street pedlar creates. Let's listen to him:

'Ladies and gentlemen, take a look at this comb, take a good look! It's a remarkable thing, ladies and gentlemen, it's not just a comb, but three combs in one that you're all going to buy from me. Look here, you see on one half of the comb, it's got thick teeth, I recommend it for those solid tangles that are difficult to smooth out; on the other half, you see the narrow teeth, marvellous for dressing the finest hair, it sweeps through it with a delightful motion. And lastly, ladies and gentlemen, on the other side of this same comb, take a look, it has no teeth at all, it's comb number three especially for the bald… Get your wallets out, ladies and gentlemen, for these *three combs in one*.' [author's translation]

If Hopkins was on dubious ground when he railed against humour in selling, Ogilvy was equally misguided to argue against 'singing your sales message'. Sometime around 1890, the young Hilaire Belloc was passing through a small town somewhere near the Pyrenees, when he heard a man singing as he walked slowly along. As Belloc approached, he saw that the man, who was about fifty, was carrying pots and pans and a kitbag, and he could make out the words of the song, which he translated to English as follows:

'Men that cook with copper know how difficult is the cleaning of copper. All cooking is a double labour unless the copper is properly tinned.'

This couplet rhymed well in the tongue he used… When he had sung this couplet once, glancing, as he sang it, nobly upwards to the left and the right at the people in their houses, he paused a little… A man in white clothes with a white square cap on his head ran out of a neighbouring door and gave him a saucepan, which he accepted with a solemn salute…

Belloc records a good deal more of the tinner's song, and then tells how he engaged the man in conversation.

Then I said, 'You sing and so advertise your trade?'

He answered, 'I do. It lifts the heart, it shortens the way, it attracts the attention of the citizens, it guarantees good work.'

'In what way,' said I, 'does it guarantee good work?'

'The man,' he answered, 'who sings loudly, clearly, and well, is a man in good health. He is master of himself. He is strict and well-managed. When people hear him they say, " Here is a prompt, ready, and serviceable man. He is not afraid. There is no rudeness in him. He is urbane, swift, and to the point. There is method in this fellow." All these things may be true of the man that does not sing, but singing makes them apparent…'

Belloc regrets he cannot offer the man something to tin, but parts from him with a compliment:

'…your singing, therefore, does not a double but a triple good. For it gives you pleasure within, it brings in trade and content from others, and it delights the world around you. It is an admirable thing.'

Belloc's account may seem over-romanticised, but it's still a tribute to a long tradition of using song, music, or humour not just to attract business, but at its best to elevate a merely commercial transaction to something that can be more rewarding and more human for all those who are involved with it.

Let's link the tinner's song, for a moment, back to the various models of advertising I presented earlier. Certainly, it contains rational sales arguments, and it attracts attention. But it also communicates non-verbal impressions about the character of the tinner, and it fosters a relationship of friendship and trust which both enables and transcends the commercial transaction at its heart. It even, according to Belloc, gives pleasure to those who overhear it, an aspiration which we might all wish more advertisers would share: not just on ethical grounds, but just as much for the practical reason that society is far more likely to tolerate advertising as long as it minimises annoyance and maximises some degree of enjoyment.

The line between those entertainers who merely seek to be rewarded for their performance, and those who use the performance as a means of selling something else, has never been distinct. Even when the performance is itself the product on sale, it needs to advertise itself, which it may do through other media, or as it often does, by giving a sample of itself. Buskers give the whole performance away first of all, and then hope to be rewarded with donations. Other traditions find that a free sample of the show is usually the best way to get people along to the paid performance, as Bonnange and Thomas have pointed out:

> [Imagine] the arrival of a circus in the village, with the elephants waddling, the acrobats turning cartwheels and the clowns making fools of themselves in the main street: these are just preliminary to the 'real' show, an advert to entice the public. But it is also, ahead of the evening performance, the circus itself putting on a show in the town.

Then, as circus owners and others have never been slow to discover, your revenue can generally be extended, sometimes a lot, by taking every opportunity to sell your audience programmes, drinks, popcorn, souvenirs, t-shirts, hats, dolls, or other merchandise. Then, why not further 'monetise' the audience you have created by selling them merchandise less and less directly related to the show itself? Whether the Pedlar at the Door first decided he could sell more ribbons if he sang and told jokes, or itinerant performers were first to realise that they could increase their income by selling ribbons rather than relying on passing the hat, is a meaningless question: entertainment and selling have always had the potential to support each other.

And the same applies when access to the audience can be profitably sold to third parties – the classic paid-for media model. Tim Wu called his fascinating book on the history of media *The Attention Merchants*, but advertisers are – or should be – buying more than mere attention when they buy space and time. Indeed, you could argue that attention in itself is hardly something that can be bought; it always has to be earned. By paying for the chance to engage with an audience that has been nurtured, generally with much effort, the advertiser is receiving only the opportunity to engage with a group who may or may not continue to be an 'audience' in the sense that was expected. No-one has put it better than that great contrarian adman, Howard Gossage:

> The buying of time or space is not the taking out of a hunting license on

someone's private preserve, but is the renting of a stage on which we may perform.

That metaphor of advertising as performance is something that is all too often forgotten. Perhaps it is because when the 'history of advertising' is written it generally focuses on the development of paid-for print media, the columns of small ads which used the technology of print and the appeal of news, even under the limitations of newspaper and advertising taxes, to circulate notices of all sorts from the seventeenth century onward. Such advertising could originally be described as mainly signposting: putting sellers in touch with buyers, employers with staff, Miss Lonelyheart with Mr Right. Yet even here an element of performance became apparent very early on, in the form of elaborate rhetoric: as Dr Johnson observed, in the somewhat tongue-in-cheek tone which literary types have so often affected when speaking of advertising,

> Advertisements are now become so numerous that they are very negligently perused, and it is therefore become necessary to gain attention by magnificence of promises, and by eloquence sometimes sublime and sometimes pathetic.

Meanwhile the histories of advertising have much less to say about the older tradition of the mountebanks, who as far as we know were to be found across Europe from the late middle ages onward, if not even earlier. In the sixteenth century Thomas Coryat wrote a detailed description of those to be seen any day in the Piazza San Marco in Venice:

> After the whole rabble of them is gotten on the stage, wherof some wear vizards [masks] being disguised like fooles in a play, some that are women… are attired with habits according to that person they sustaine; after (I say) they are all upon the stage, the music begins.

During the performance, which included comedy, music, and tricks, the quack doctor would bring out vials and potions from his trunk on stage, and then begin a sales pitch which was, above all, designed to be as entertaining as possible:

> …these Naturall Orators… would tell their tales with such admirable volubility and plausible grace, even extempore, and seasoned with that singular variety

of elegant jests and witty conceits, that they did often strike admiration into strangers that never heard them before: and by how much the more eloquent these Naturalists are, by so much the greater audience they draw unto them, *and the more ware they sell.* [emphasis added]

It's remarkable how this basic formula – music, costumes, humour, antics, and a sales pitch disguised as witty banter – seems to have persisted through the centuries and across geographies. By 1772 mountebanks had already become such a nuisance in the American states (at least in the eyes of their puritan leaders) that both New Jersey and Connecticut passed stern legislation against them. Despite this, the performances continued to delight the crowds whenever they could get away with it. As the nineteenth century saw massive increases in the US population, unimagined improvements in transport and communications, and the beginnings of mass production, such shows became more and more common; so, although its origins go back much earlier, the heyday of the travelling 'medicine show' was from about 1870 to the 1930s, only fading away as the advent of commercial broadcast radio increasingly offered what was, basically, a very similar formula, but delivered direct to your own living room.

The medicine shows, as the name suggests, primarily made their money by selling a wide range of potions, elixirs, and remedies of all kinds. Most ordinary people had limited access to medical care, and in any case the treatments 'officially' on offer were themselves little different from those of centuries earlier – bleeding, cupping, starving, and drugs with dangerous side effects – so the demand for cures was almost universal. On the supply side, the manufacture of medicines and the claims that could be made for them were almost entirely unregulated before the early twentieth century, so the cost of making them was generally kept very low. The products on offer could be essentially harmless coloured water (which might after all have a placebo effect), though they often silently contained opium, laudanum, cocaine, or alcohol, any of which might induce a feeling of momentary well-being, as well as longer term damage or addiction. In a few cases, there might even have been folk remedies of some real merit.

Medicine show troupes ranged in size from the travelling individual to teams of thirty or forty performers and salespeople, operating on a national scale. At the lower end of the business the sellers might buy in stock from wholesalers, and lived hand to mouth by selling it on for what they could get, but the larger and more evolved organisations quickly realised there was much more long term profit to be made by creating a brand. This was partly to protect their own identity as a travelling show – it was all too easy for impostors to show up in town claiming to be the genuine 'Kickapoo Indians' or whatever. But more importantly, a branded product could be supplied permanently to the local shopkeepers and a continual stream of sales generated long after the show itself had left town. The more successful shows made most of their money this way – the product was sold at the show itself as a heavily discounted trial offer, while the full price paid for repeat purchases supported a healthy margin both for the manufacturer and the retailer. This had the added benefit of keeping the local shopkeepers on side, who otherwise might regard the travelling show as stealing their business. Hence, brands of patent medicine such as Hamlin's Wizard Oil, Kickapoo Indian Oil or Buffalo Salve, Wahoo Bitters, or Ka-Ton-Ka anticipated many of the basic techniques of packaged goods marketing: the distinctive brand, discounts for accelerating trial, the importance of distribution and repeat purchase.

The typical medicine show itself was not unlike the mountebanks Coryat saw in sixteenth century Venice: a basic combination of music and comedy sketches, with the added options of conjuring tricks, acrobatics, or performing animals. There might be a small charge for the show, or it might be free; sometimes a special performance with less sales pitches might be priced more highly (an early example of premium pricing to 'go ad free'). The entertainment would be interrupted by sales pitches, with carefully choreographed opportunities to buy – the pitchmen would normally claim they only had a limited stock available, and encourage the audience to part with their money with frequent shouts of 'running out over here!' to each other. (This device, which Robert Cialdini called the Scarcity Principle, will be familiar to anyone today who books, say, hotel rooms online – 'Only two rooms left at this venue!'.)

The actual sales pitch needed to be entertaining enough to hold the audience's goodwill, but was also a chance to switch from the mode of pure entertainment to a more serious and quasi-scientific exposition of the products, supported with testimonials and demonstrations wherever possible. So we can see in these outlines, patterns that would later recur in broadcast media – the commercial break within the programme, the 'science bit' within the commercial.

The medicine show faced increasing challenges in the twentieth century. The US Food and Drugs Act of 1905 began to regulate the sale of patent medicines. First the cinema, and then radio, offered alternative sources of entertainment; the automobile enabled the rural market to travel further and choose their own pastimes. Given all this, it is perhaps surprising that the last shows persisted until around 1950, when the advent of television proved the final straw. But the principles that had supported the medicine show and its antecedents lived on. As Brooks McNamara concludes in his classic history of the medicine show, *Step Right Up*:

> The premise of the medicine show was that a free performance would sell a product. The premise was a sound one and radio and television merely borrowed it and developed it on a scale far beyond anything dreamt of by the travelling medicine showman.

This kind of history, however, is precisely what led admen like Hopkins and Ogilvy to frame advertising in a completely different way. In their compulsion to present advertising as a serious, technically expert profession, advertising practitioners took every opportunity to distance themselves from the legacy of street performers and fraudulent remedies, Wizard Oil, and Barnum and Bailey's Circus. When David Ogilvy inveighed against 'singing your sales message', was he perhaps thinking of a passage like the following, from *The Hucksters*?

> The Old Man [the client] looked amused. "Only a singer you say, Mr Norman. Well, I want you to know that the Beautee Soap Company thinks singers are mighty important. And I'll tell you why, Mr Norman."
>
> He opened the drawer of the table and triumphantly held aloft a bar of Beautee Soap.
>
> "Because singers can sell soap, Mr Norman. Right, Kimberley?"
>
> "RIGHT," said Kimberley.

Kimberley, as you might guess, is the agency Yes-man. And the Old Man – a figure based on the appalling George Washington Hill of the American Tobacco

Company – is an arrogant bully. But – to use the words Bill Bernbach used to carry on a card in his pocket – perhaps he's right? Maybe the business of selling stuff – and more importantly, the business of building profitable brands – has a good deal more to do with entertainment and popular culture than the advertising profession has usually liked to admit.

*

In these opening chapters I have reviewed various practitioner models of how advertising works, and observed that the dominant theories of 'message transmission' or 'rational persuasion' are often less important in reality than the ability to charm, to entertain, and to create fame. We have also looked at the historical roots of how the advertising and marketing professions came to distance themselves culturally from the vulgar, carnival worlds of Barnum and the medicine show, while still continuing, in practice, to use their techniques.

Yet this disdained carnival world still creates the basis not just for advertising, but for the long term profitability of successful brands. In the next section, we'll look in more detail at how the fame-creating techniques of P.T. Barnum laid the foundations for the growth of manufacturer brands in the nineteenth century – and how much brands and celebrities have in common.

Part Two

A Kind of Fame

I fell in with the world's way; and if my 'puffing' was more persistent, my advertising more audacious, my posters more glaring, my pictures more exaggerated, my flags more patriotic and my transparencies more brilliant than they would have been under the management of my neighbours, it was not because I had less scruple than they, but more energy, far more ingenuity, and a better foundation for such promises.

PHINEAS T. BARNUM

Coca-Cola became a go because it was pushed and pushed by an energetic man. If the Pembertons had not sold the formula it probably would have stayed in an old drink somewhere and been lost in time.

A RELATIVE OF 'DOC' PEMBERTON, QUOTED IN *FOR GOD, COUNTRY, AND COCA-COLA*

Just about the only thing that successful brands have in common is a kind of fame.

JEREMY BULLMORE

Chapter Five

From Barnum to Brands

O n September 1st, 1850, the wharves of downtown New York were packed with crowds. A bower of trees decorated with flags, and two triumphal arches topped with eagles had also appeared overnight on the quay. Everyone cheered wildly as the steamship *Atlantic* approached, with two contrasting figures conspicuous on her deck, a young woman and a somewhat older man. Jenny Lind, the 'Swedish Nightingale' was at the end of the long voyage from London; Phineas Taylor Barnum had just joined the ship at the Verrazano Narrows to welcome the famous singer.

Jenny Lind was not yet thirty years old, but already had a major reputation in Europe as an operatic soprano. By most accounts, she did have a fine voice and great musicality. She had recently however chosen to leave the operatic stage due to religious scruples – theatrical performances were still widely seen as tainted with immorality. Her concert programmes would still contain a few operatic arias, but more folksongs, novelty pieces, and popular numbers like 'Home Sweet Home'.

Although Barnum had never met Lind before this moment, nor heard her sing, he had stretched himself to the financial limit to promote her first concert tour of the United States. Her contracted fee of $1,000 for each of 150 scheduled appearances had already been lodged with Barings Bank in London, together with smaller fees for the music director and baritone soloist who would support her, and as well as all this Barnum was paying for the venue hire and all the expenses of the tour. Although he was already a successful impresario, he had had to sell several properties and borrow extensively to get to this point. Barnum could not afford this tour to fail.

Despite her reputation in Europe, Lind was much less known in the USA, so Barnum had been working for the best part of a year to build her fame, using all the techniques of publicity he had already perfected in promoting his previous acts. These had included Joice Heth, supposedly the 160 year old nurse of George Washington; Colonel Tom Thumb, a dwarf entertainer whom Barnum had presented to Queen Victoria; and the notorious 'Feejee Mermaid', a laughable confection of a dead monkey and mummified fish, which had nevertheless become a national sensation.

As he had done with these, Barnum waged a sustained campaign of creating 'news' about Jenny Lind which the newspapers could not resist amplifying. The London *Times* described his pioneering P.R. techniques:

> He invented what we may call for want of a better name the police of puffery. He had actually, for months before Jenny Lind's arrival, a number of provocative agents, as the French call them, in his pay, whose business was to 'get up a *furore*' for Jenny Lind. This *furore* once excited, was chronicled by the newspapers, and thus infinitely multiplied, as heat and light are increased by being reflected (Cook, p.200).

Biographies, prints, and the newfangled daguerreotypes of Jenny were all widely on sale, and through such methods Barnum spun a consistent myth not just about the incredible beauty of Jenny Lind's voice, but her purity of soul, her humble beginnings in the Swedish countryside, and her devoted work for charity. Barnum's own established fame as a showman, and the unprecedented ambitiousness of the tour, added to the newsworthiness of the story. Tickets for the first performance in each city had been ostentatiously auctioned, with prodigious sums paid by those who wished to promote themselves or their businesses by spending the most money – the highest price was $650, in Boston, paid by a popular singer called Ossian Dodge. By the time Lind stepped off the ship in New York, surrounded by those cheering crowds (who like everything else were almost certainly organised by Barnum himself), the foundations of 'Lindomania' had been well laid.

If Barnum deserves his lasting reputation as 'the greatest showman' and 'the prince of humbugs' it is not so much because he did things that had never been done before, but that he did them with greater energy and on a much greater scale than anyone else, at a moment in time when advances in communications and transport were making that scale possible: the rise of mass circulation newspapers, colour printing and photography, the railroad and the steamship. In one of the many versions of his autobiography, Barnum would later write that:

> It was the world's way then, as it is now, to excite the community with flaming posters, promising almost everything for next to nothing… I fell in with the world's way; and if my 'puffing' was more persistent, my advertising more audacious, my posters more glaring, my pictures more exaggerated, my flags more patriotic and my transparencies more brilliant than they would have been under the management of my neighbours, it was not because I had less scruple than they, but more energy, far more ingenuity, and a better foundation for such promises (Lears, p.267).

By taking a massive gamble on Jenny Lind, Barnum was consciously aiming to widen his appeal to the 'respectable' classes. But his techniques remained essentially the same as those he had used for his more lowbrow projects. The appeal of 'Lindomania', which continued to grow throughout the tour, was not confined to the well-off middle classes who could afford the tickets for the Swedish Nightingale's actual performances (often the cheapest tickets were priced at $3 or $4, a whole week's wages for most working class people at the time). Frequently, large crowds of the less well-off would gather outside the concert halls, hoping to hear something of the performance, or merely to catch a glimpse of the angelic Jenny. Sometimes these assemblies became unruly, as in Cincinnati, where windows were broken and pistols fired, while the terrified singer retreated to her dressing room. More profitably, an immense range of Jenny Lind merchandise had something to appeal to all classes: the wealthy could find Jenny Lind pianos or riding hats on Broadway, while women in the plebeian neighbourhoods of Canal Street or The Bowery flocked to buy Jenny Lind plaids, combs, silks, ear-rings, work baskets, bonnets and hair pins, and their men folk chewed Jenny Lind tobacco and smoked Jenny Lind cigars. In these ways, huge numbers of Americans who could never dream of affording a concert ticket could buy their own admission to 'Lindomania'.

It would be simplistic to claim Jenny Lind as the first modern 'celebrity' – nothing about her promotion was without precedent, and you could make a case for Colonel Tom Thumb, or indeed Barnum himself, as having got there first. But she stands as a good example of how future celebrities would develop. There had been many famous performers before, but her fame was arguably out of all proportion to her actual importance, as the London *Times* disapprovingly wrote at the time:

> It is humiliating to see a nation which boasts that it leads the van of human improvement so little capable of appreciating the relative dignity and merit of human talents and employments as to bow down in prostrate admiration at the feet of a woman who, after all, is merely a first rate vocalist…(Cook, p.200)

But the engineering of fame has never been constrained by such value judgments, being in this case (as most often) driven by purely commercial considerations. Barnum was in it to make money, and having wagered much, he did make a great deal more. The tour was not without internal strains or public controversy, but for the most part the large venues that Barnum had hired were well filled, and the ticket prices remained high. The Nightingale travelled down the eastern seaboard, then gave several concerts in Havana before returning via New Orleans and up the Mississippi and Missouri by steamboat. After 93 performances, rather than the planned 150, both Lind and Barnum were increasingly tired (and tired of each other) and the contract was mutually dissolved, but each had already made a fortune from the project. Jenny married and changed her name; as Mme. Goldschmidt she continued to perform in the USA for a couple more years before returning to Europe, but she never enjoyed the same degree of fame as she had under Barnum's management. Barnum returned to his many other enterprises, such as the Museums which he already owned in New York. A little later, he founded the travelling circus of Barnum and Bailey, 'the Greatest Show on Earth', for which he bought, from the London Zoo, Jumbo the elephant – who would become a celebrity bigger (in all senses) than the Swedish Nightingale.

But the greatest celebrity that Barnum created was Barnum himself. Always a tireless self-publicist, he wrote and published autobiographical and other works throughout his career, lectured extensively both on temperance (he was a teetotaller) and on the art of making money, and never missed an opportunity to associate himself with his creations – as in that moment when he had appeared on deck with Jenny Lind at her arrival in New York. In his home town of Bridgeport, Connecticut, he built a palatial house for himself in the style of the Brighton Pavilion, which he named 'Iranistan'; its picture appeared widely, and Jenny Lind later admitted that seeing a print of it on Barnum's headed notepaper had decided her to choose Barnum rather than a rival impresario. As early as the 1840s, when it was used as the title for a farce at New York's Burton's Theatre, 'Where's Barnum?' had become a universal catchphrase for any novelty. When Barnum claimed, shortly before he died, to be the most famous person in the world, he may well have been correct. Yet as far as we can tell his motive for maintaining his personal fame was essentially commercial; he well understood that 'brand Barnum' had value, and towards the end of his life he still demanded that his partners pay him $10,000 a year as royalty for the use of his name, while he retained the right to use it on other enterprises.

It was only a matter of time before the principles of creating celebrity on a mass scale would be emulated by others, in other contexts.

*

> If this business were to be split up, I would be glad to take the brands, trademarks, and good will, and you could have all the bricks and mortar – and I would fare better than you.

If you've read anything about brands, you have probably come across these words, attributed to John Stuart of The Quaker Oats Company. Perhaps, as I did, you have wondered at some point who John Stuart was, when he lived, and – given the amount of falsely attributed quotations that circulate the internet – whether he ever really said them.

Not everyone seems to have been so curious. John Murphy, the founder of Interbrand, attributes them in his fascinating autobiography *Brandfather* to 'John Stuart, Chairman, Quaker, 1990 [sic]'. Jan Lindemann, in the Economist book *Brands and Branding*, quotes a slightly garbled version and identifies John Stuart as 'Chairman of Quaker, circa 1900'.

Neither is close to the correct date. John Stuart was born in 1877, the son of Robert Stuart who co-founded the Quaker Oats Company in 1901. Having worked his way up through the business, he became President in 1922 at the age of 45, and Chairman twenty years later; he remained a director of the company until 1964, and died in 1969. According to the 1967 official history of the Quaker Oats Company, which appears to be the original source of the quote, the famous words were spoken by Stuart over lunch to the man who would succeed him as President, Donold B. Lourie. The date of the conversation is not recorded, but as Lourie recalls it as 'early in his career', it was most likely during the 1920s or 1930s, when Stuart was still President. The quote was regarded as sufficiently important by the author of the company history, Arthur Marquette, that he not only used it to close the book, but referenced it for his title – *Brands, Trademarks, and Goodwill*.

There are two reasons why it's worth locating this quote accurately. Firstly, it demonstrates that a serious business concern with the value of brand names is not a recent invention (as John Murphy's fanciful date might imply). Secondly, it invites us to consider the context in which Stuart made such a confident assertion, by looking in a bit more detail at the history of the Quaker Oats Company itself – a story which demonstrates how and why brand names and trademarks became so important from the last decades of the nineteenth century onward.

*

The eventual emergence of The Quaker Oats Company in 1901 was the outcome of a twenty years' power struggle between three men, and more fundamentally between radically different strategies for achieving profitable domination of a growing market.

During the last decades of the nineteenth century, the urban population of the United States was increasing rapidly. City dwellers had neither time nor appetite for the heavy breakfasts traditional among rural workers, so were increasingly prepared to choose oatmeal as a nutritious and easy alternative. Oat growing and milling flourished in the rich agricultural lands of Ohio, Iowa, and Illinois.

For the most part this was a commodity market, the milled oats being shipped to general stores in barrels where the proprietor would sell them by the pound. As a commodity, it was subject to frequent fluctuations in market prices, which over time tended to benefit the largest producers who could both survive the bad times and produce at the lowest cost. Over time, this led to many smaller millers being swallowed up by the bigger firms, and then to various attempts to establish some kind of cartel or 'trust' which would artificially control prices – at that time, still a legal procedure. None succeeded, but in 1888 seven large mills combined to form the American Cereal Company. This would prosper during the following decade under the severely conflicted leadership of three, very different, mill owners – a power struggle that was based not just on personal differences, but on fundamentally different beliefs about business strategy. The three men were Ferdinand Schumacher, Henry Crowell, and Robert Stuart.

Schumacher was of German peasant stock, with a lined face and an Amish-like beard, tough, uncompromising, and old enough to be father of the other two. He had previously dominated the commodity market, and was known as the 'King of Oatmeal' – because of this he ended up with a controlling interest of more than 50% in American Cereal. He had always run his business as a traditional low-cost producer, and having always prospered by doing so, he saw no other way.

Henry Parsons Crowell could not have been more different: from a wealthy family, and deeply religious, he only worked because he believed it was God's will that he should do something useful for mankind. In 1881 Crowell had bought a bankrupt mill in Ravenna, Ohio, whose previous owner had registered the trade mark of 'a man in Quaker garb' as a badge of identification. Crowell made great use of this image, pioneering the practice of pre-packaging his rolled oats in cardboard cartons pre-printed in colours with the Quaker trade mark, and advertising it extensively.

Robert Stuart, of Scottish descent by way of Ontario, owned mills in Chicago and Cedar Rapids, Ohio. A long time friend and ally of Crowell, he became secretary-treasurer of American Cereal while Crowell was Vice-President. Schumacher, as the majority shareholder, had appointed himself President.

There was continual friction between Schumacher and Crowell, principally on the topic of advertising. Schumacher believed advertising was a foolish waste of money, while Crowell saw it as the only strategy that would ensure the company's future survival. Already it was becoming clear that anti-trust laws were likely to make any kind of cartel or monopoly illegal, and that the only way to 'own' market share would be through the mind of the consumer. The two men could only just about co-exist because they continued to market two different brands of rolled oats – Schumacher's old label 'F.S' (for his initials), and Crowell's Quaker Oats.

While F.S Oats were modestly supported with the occasional staid press ad, Quaker Oats were promoted with ever increasing sums in all possible ways. The distinctive visual trademark

> ...blazed from the sides of buildings, illuminated billboards at eye-vantage points carefully chosen in crowded districts, caught the gaze of streetcar riders from car cards, and flashed unexpectedly from the news columns of daily papers from coast to coast. Metal signs were hung on rural fences facing roads; gold letters were glued to grocery store windows and doors. Calendars, blotters, dodgers, and cookbooks deluged the mails...advertisements were placed in select groups of magazines. Week long cooking schools were held in grocery stores after little boys had been hired to placard every house in the neighbourhood... Important county, state, and national fairs and expositions found Quaker represented with a booth that dispensed free samples, the public being appraised of the Quaker location by brilliantly coloured postcards of pretty children, nostalgic scenes, and other souvenir-value pictures.

To introduce Quaker Oats to the Pacific North-west, Crowell chartered a fifteen coach train; an advance man recruited from a circus went from town to town ahead of it to create excitement and buy space in local papers. When thousands of local people had been lured to each station, the train would arrive with a demonstration and entertainment, a six foot figure of the 'man in Quaker garb' atop the engine, while free samples were given out to all.

These techniques were all derived from the practices of travelling entertainers, circuses and medicine shows, and the sensational exhibitions toured by P.T. Barnum. These historical links with patent medicines and popular entertainment had given advertising a somewhat disreputable image among respectable manufacturers. Henry Crowell was one of the first to change that by demonstrating that, basically, it worked. His ballyhoo created demand – when his sales force eventually visited the retailers, they had already had many customers asking for the product by name, and were only too keen to order.

By 1897 Crowell was spending $500,000 a year on advertising. (To put this into context, in 1900 Coca-Cola was still only spending $85,000). The business had grown enormously as a result, but Schumacher was still convinced it would have happened anyway. In 1898 the conflict between the directors came to a head, and in a boardroom coup Schumacher ousted the other two men. The next two years, by cutting advertising, he was able to post record profits, apparently justifying his own approach. But the growth had stalled, and Schumacher was no longer investing in either marketing or production. Crowell and Stuart began quietly buying American Cereal stock, and eventually in 1899, through a complex series of manoeuvres, managed to regain control of the company. Schumacher finally allowed himself to be bought out (at a price) and retired. The business was soon reconstituted under the name of The Quaker Oats Company.

The new management at once began to reinvest. By 1901 sales were nearly $16m, up by 25% from 1898, and profits over $1m for the first time. By 1910 sales were $25m and profits over $2m. In an era when anti-trust laws had now become reality, Crowell and Stuart had demonstrated that

> Success in oatmeal marketing lay in a distinctive trademark, the product packaged for purity and ease of handling, and nationally sold on a consumer franchise gained by advertising.

Crowell's promotions, like those of his contemporary William Hesketh Lever who was then pioneering similar techniques in the UK for marketing soap, came in a myriad of forms. (As far as we can tell Crowell directed most of the 'creative' work himself, and certainly didn't use an ad agency at this time.) One of his principles was to keep people's interest through continual novelty: 'What will those Quaker people think of next?'. There were rational arguments for the nutritious qualities of oats and purity of manufacture, there were humorous stories and poems, there were children's cartoon books, there were calendars and useful merchandise of all kinds, there was sampling and there was ubiquitous outdoor presence, there were stunts and events and carnival floats and sponsorships, and box top promotional offers. Some of it was serious, much was trivial or fanciful. But what held it all together was the name and the evolving trademark of 'the man in Quaker garb', who over the years became plumper, more smiley, and more stylised. In other words, the single factor behind the growth of Quaker Oats – and the same would be true of Sunlight Soap, or of most other brands of the period – was simply the creation of fame.

Although he would not have recognised the phrase 'mental availability', Crowell seems to have understood the principle perfectly; he also understood that the way to deliver this was through a combination of endless variety including much entertainment, consistent use of the distinctive device of the Quaker Man, and consistently large advertising budgets. The outcomes for the business were stable market share, stable distribution, and improved prices, which in turn funded both more advertising and the ability to invest in quality improvement and innovation.

*

In putting together the stories of Jenny Lind and Quaker Oats, I have been trying to suggest that, from the early days of mass communications and popular culture, brands and celebrities have had much in common, and have been created by similar techniques – principally the use of mass media, combined with novelty, attractiveness, compelling narratives, and the use of distinctive assets, to maximise mental availability.

But I am not the first person to liken brands to celebrities. In 2001 Jeremy Bullmore (formerly Creative Director, and later Chairman of J Walter Thompson, London) gave a typically wise and insightful lecture to the British Brands Group under the catchy title 'Posh Spice and Persil'. The juxtaposition of a leading UK brand of washing powder with the Spice Girl, Victoria Beckham, was inspired by a line in her recently-published autobiography, *Learning to Fly*:

Right from the beginning, I said I wanted to be more famous than Persil Automatic (p.123).

It may not be surprising that young Victoria Adams, smitten by the musical *Fame* at an early age before she pursued her ambition to go to stage school, set her personal goal in terms of fame. What was more intriguing for Jeremy was her point of comparison:

> It was very astute of the young Posh Spice to choose not Robbie Williams nor Sir Cliff Richard nor Madonna as her benchmark of fame but the country's best-known washing powder.

> Because just about the only thing that successful brands have in common is a kind of fame. Indeed, it's been suggested that brands are the real celebrities. And for most human beings, fame not only holds a powerful fascination but bestows an incalculable value on anything that enjoys it. We value the famous far more highly than the little known.

There are important connections and synergies between brands and celebrities, as well as similarities. Jenny Lind was used to sell a wide range of merchandise (though it's not clear how much of this trade was actually controlled by Barnum or Lind), while 'Mr Quaker' had some of the characteristics of an actual person. These synergies have continued right up to the present, and have perhaps never been more striking than they are today. Celebrities have been, and are, used to sell brands; brand publicity enhances the fame of celebrities; brands create their own characters, who become quasi-celebrities; and today, more than ever, celebrities create their own brands. George Clooney, David Beckham, Alexandr Orlov the Meerkat, Kylie Jenner, and countless others past and present, are all part of a long established ecosystem in which personal and commercial fame are not just mutually supportive, but often difficult to tell apart.

Yet while brands have become a central concept in the marketing lexicon, the concept of fame and the character of the celebrity remain less respected and even less respectable. Why might this be?

The word *celebrity* was originally a synonym for *fame*, but its use to mean 'a person of celebrity' dates back to 1849, and in the twentieth century this has become its principal sense. Daniel Boorstin, in his 1961 book *The Image*, wrote a critical yet perceptive chapter in which he famously defined a celebrity as 'a person who is known for his well-knownness':

> He is neither good nor bad, great nor petty. He is the human pseudo-event. He has been fabricated on purpose to satisfy our exaggerated expectations of human greatness. He is morally neutral... He is made by all of us who willingly read about him, who like to see him on television, who buy recordings of his voice, and talk about him to our friends. His relation to morality and even to reality is highly ambiguous (p.58).

In the context of this kind of disparaging language, it is not surprising that modern marketers of brands have preferred to ignore the many parallels between celebrities and brands. Yet in reality, what they do is fundamentally very similar to all this. And, stripped of its tendentious contrasts between the decadence of modern fame and the genuinely admirable, deserving 'heroes' of past ages, Boorstin's chapter points to some important truths about fame.

Fame does not automatically reward the most deserving, the noblest human being or the greatest performer, or the finest hamburger or even the most user-friendly website. It is basically a simple matter of scale – of reaching enough people, of being appealing enough to interest and attract them even though this may be in the most trivial of ways, of being distinctive enough to be memorable, and as a result of all this to become talked about, shared, argued over, as part of a shared language or culture.

Boorstin's line about the celebrity being 'well-known for his well-knownness' is unfair, but also contains a deeper truth. I tend to agree with Jeremy Bullmore that, to begin with at least, any celebrity or brand must be famous '*for* something' – even though that something may not be a quality or distinction much valued by a college professor like Boorstin. Celebrities have based fame on chance appearances on talent shows, or on bit parts in TV commercials, or on merely being a cat with a grumpy face. But the more important insight behind Boorstin's jibe is that once you are famous, that fame exists independently of its original trigger, and it's possible to transfer the fame to something quite different. Victoria Beckham was a pop singer, and is now a fashion designer;

her husband David went from footballer to style icon (and unofficial member of the royal family); Donald Trump ... well, we all know about him. The same is true of brands. Apple, Amazon, Google, all now make most of their profits from products or services that were never thought of when they first became famous. More fundamentally, a strategy of maintaining 'well-knownness' enables a greater scope for action and innovation, greater access to resources, and above all, greater potential for continuing to build more fame. Fame is, in short, an asset, and, as with money, the more you have, the easier it is to get access to more.

Yet none of this happens automatically, or even predictably. Fame can be – indeed, generally has to be – managed: but it can never be controlled. For every brand or individual or film or record that achieves large scale fame, countless thousands fail, and for every one that maintains lasting fame over decades, thousands more flourish only for months or weeks or days.

So fame has a reputation for being unpredictable, unfair, morally suspect – and, perhaps worst of all, intimately associated with the world of popular culture and popular entertainment from which the advertising and marketing communities have for so long struggled to distance themselves. It's perhaps not surprising, then, that the word plays a relatively small part in the marketing lexicon. I can trace a few mentions, mostly recent. Sir Nigel Bogle, one of the founders of BBH, once described his agency as 'a fame factory'. Les Binet and Peter Field, in their invaluable analyses of IPA Effectiveness Awards winning cases (2007), conclude that campaigns which have a strategy based on 'fame' are more successful than any others. The ad research company System1 base their measurements of ads on three qualities which they call 'Fame, Feeling, and Fluency' . And Bob Hoffman, who always goes straight to the heart of the matter, wrote a wonderful blog post called 'The Problem with Bubba's Burgers' in which he explains why

> ...the simplest and most obvious objective of marketing should be to create fame. Brands that are famous have an enormous advantage over brands that aren't famous.

But mostly, the word 'fame' is conspicuous by its absence. It doesn't appear in the indexes of any of the advertising textbooks I own, and it doesn't feature much in citations for awards or in case histories. 'Making the brand famous' seldom appears as a strategy or creative brief, although we often dance around it with words like 'brand awareness' or 'brand image' – or even, today, 'mental availability'. Byron Sharp has good reasons for using a precise, unemotional phrase like 'mental availability' for his evidence-based argument, but in the ad business we should be used to the idea that words have connotative as well as denotative meanings. So 'fame', while it's close in literal meaning to 'mental availability', evokes a different world – and it's precisely this different world, the world of popular entertainment and celebrity, which is central to understanding brands and advertising, and which at the same time has been consistently sidelined by advertising agencies and marketing departments. After all, Victoria Adams did not set out on her showbiz career with a dream to have the same 'brand awareness' as a leading detergent. And, so far at least, no-one has written a hit musical called *Mental Availability*.

We saw in the story of Sunny Jim how, from the 1900s onward, advertising agencies carefully constructed a 'professional' persona that aimed to protect their turf from incursions by mere entertainers or 'amateurs'. Part of this involved elaborate theories of advertising as 'salesmanship', models of rational persuasion which only admitted entertainment, if at all, as a means to the supposedly higher end of communicating 'product benefits'. The Force case history was frequently repeated over decades because it seemed to show that frivolous fame was not as effective as serious selling – a conclusion that, as we have seen, was not justified. It's true that fame alone doesn't invariably lead to sustainable business success – lack of physical availability, or a downright inadequate product or service, can scupper a brand's potential. Yet the converse of this is more important – in most circumstances, fame is the core dimension on which nearly every brand succeeds competitively.

Let's return to Jeremy Bullmore's words:

> ... for most human beings, fame not only holds a powerful fascination but bestows an incalculable value on anything that enjoys it. We value the famous far more highly than the little known.

We could find psychological theories to support this assertion: Kahneman's 'availability heuristic' posits that we prefer things that come to mind easily, and the theory of social proof described by Cialdini and others says that we tend to want what we see lots of other people wanting . Sociologists would argue that we 'value the famous' for other reasons too; anything famous creates a shared reference point for social exchange, which offers us the many pleasures of talking about it, disparaging it, arguing about it, joining the fan club or getting up a petition against it, and so on. By engaging with what is famous, we gain admittance to a social group which may offer acceptance, validation, a sense of belonging. But it is unlikely that P.T. Barnum, Henry Crowell, or Victoria Adams paid conscious attention to such theories; they just understood, at first intuitively and very soon from experience, that fame is the basis for business success on a large scale.

If we entertain the theory that brand success is primarily driven by fame, it makes additional sense of the pervasive links between advertising, brands, and entertainment that we have been considering previously. Fame is a good word for the common factor which informs the entire eco-system of mass media, popular culture, and brands. And the factors that make celebrities or films or songs or TV shows famous are not very different from those that make brands famous and therefore successful.

Yet this is very different from the conventional thinking that has grown up around brands. Just as the ad industry constructed theories of advertising which were based on rational persuasion rather than entertainment, marketers have, over the last fifty years, built up a complicated and esoteric body of theories about how brands succeed which are now generally regarded as dogma. These include the doctrines of *brand essence, brand positioning, brand personality, brand benefits*, and, most fashionably in the past decade, *brand purpose*. These concepts have been combined together in a bewildering variety of graphic devices, such as brand prisms, brand pyramids, brand temples, brand keys and, most notoriously, the brand onion. Perhaps in an attempt to reduce this complexity to simplicity again, it is also commonly asserted that a brand can only succeed if it can formulate a clear, single minded, and unique 'essence' or 'purpose', together with a detailed specification for how every aspect of the brand's behaviour should be closely directed. This 'essentialist' or 'Platonic' view of brands was typically summed up by Jez Frampton, then Global CEO of Interbrand, in the Economist book *Brands and Branding* (Second Edition, 2009):

> Great brands are defined by their relevance and distinctiveness, by that *single-minded proposition* that places them in the hearts and minds of consumers… Behind every brand is a compelling *idea*, which captures customers' attention and loyalty by filling an unmet or unsatisfied need… (*emphasis added*, p.62)

This is the orthodoxy repeated throughout academia, for example in this online prospectus for the City College of New York's course 'Branding and Integrated Communications':

> At the heart of virtually every successful organization is a clearly defined and broadly understood brand idea. Whether called a 'Brand Driver,' 'Brand DNA,' 'Brand Essence' or similar, it is invariably [sic] the central, unifying concept or maxim that converts business strategy into desired corporate behavior, driving product and service development, employee engagement and conduct and all marketing communications.

This kind of formulation does not mention fame, nor does it acknowledge the context of popular culture and media in which brands live or die. In this world, any successful brand is assumed to grow and survive, not by a process of adaptation and response to a complex environment, but on the pure and abstract basis of some essence or idea unique to itself which somehow informs all its actions, and which the consumer cannot obtain elsewhere.

However convoluted they often are, essentialist theories of brands start from the assumption that brands become successful because of *what they are*, rather than *what they do* – and this is the wrong way round. Brands, like celebrities, become successful, as a general rule, as they become famous. Jenny Lind did not become famous because she was the best singer, or even because of her supposedly unique beauty or personality (though all these represented elements in the stories that were spun about her) – she became as famous as she did because Barnum knew how to promote her. Quaker Oats dominated the oatmeal category not because it was a superior product or even because it was unusual in sporting an attractive visual trademark – there were plenty such, including King, Snowdrift, North

Maid, Rose Queen, Lakeland, and so on – but because Henry Crowell followed the techniques of Barnum in making sure the brand became and stayed more famous than any of these others.

Essentialist theories about brands contain an element of truth. There is a sense in which brands can develop, and can aspire to direct, consistent 'personalities' , 'images', or even 'purposes'. Barnum projected a carefully constructed image for Jenny Lind, and that was a significant part of her appeal. Yet the essentialist view, as it has become entrenched in conventional wisdom at least, seems to assume that if you construct a sufficiently compelling personality or narrative, the rest will take care of itself. This leaves out three important dimensions:

+ The first is that any image or story or product, no matter how attractive, will only achieve fame if it can command access to mass audiences, over time.

+ The second is that without sufficiently fluent distinctiveness, or uniqueness, the attractive story cannot be owned.

+ And the third is that, whatever the plans or intentions of the brand managers, the image or narrative that will achieve both media coverage and popular involvement is never entirely predictable, but continually emerges from the interaction between the brand's own intention, the public response, and external events of all kinds.

As I re-read Jeremy Bullmore's lecture on brands and fame, I found myself becoming curious as to how 'Posh Spice' herself had become so famous. The young Victoria Adams may have been ambitious for fame, but how did she actually achieve it? I was right to suppose that she did not have a multi-million pound budget for advertising, like Persil Automatic did. So what was the sequence of events that led to her becoming such a leading celebrity, when so many thousands of other stage school hopefuls remain unknown, or have enjoyed at best a short spell in the public mind?

Is it because she has always had personal qualities and skills that destined her irrevocably for success? Did she, or others on her behalf, set out with a clear idea for what her essence or image should be? Or did she just get lucky? Certainly both personal qualities and some luck were involved. But the story of what happened also demonstrates how the intrinsic qualities or talents of a celebrity or brand can be much less important in creating fame than reaching mass audiences, creating distinctiveness, and perhaps above all, responding creatively to unplanned events.

Chapter Six

David Beckham's Sarong

It's easy enough to look at the events which led to Victoria Adams becoming famous: copies of *Learning to Fly* are available online today for a few pence each, and it's an interesting read. It's true that this is a partial account, telling Victoria's side of the story, but we can cross refer to Andrew Morton's catty little book from a year earlier, *Posh and Becks*, and find the salient details not very different.

The overall narrative arc through the first half of the book is one common in celebrity memoirs – the years of struggle, frustration, and rejection, eventually leading to the Big Break. Young Victoria is told at her stage school she's too fat to be in the end of term shows, she perseveres through years of training and auditions that lead to nothing, she has one decent gig in a musical that flops after a trial run in Birmingham, she takes exploitative jobs handing out leaflets in shopping centres. Then one day she sees a small ad: 'Girl singers wanted for pop group'. Is this 'the big break'? But no, this turns out to be another dead end, so after a while she answers *another* ad which leads her to father and son promoters, Bob and Chris Herbert. She and a few other girls are chosen from hundreds who audition, and the Herberts pay them to spend time together working on an act with them.

This is where it gets more interesting. The Spice Girls always had a reputation as a manufactured band. But what gradually happens over time, once the line up has settled down to the final five, is that the young women themselves have increasingly strong views about the material they want to do, and what they want to be. Bob and Chris want to call the band 'Touch'. They tell them they don't like it. Then Geri comes up with the name 'Spice'. They start to write their own material, including their first hit, 'Wannabe'. But they've never signed a proper contract with Bob and Chris, and after two years they steal the tape of their songs and leave (they later pay them back for all the money they invested in them).

The group, now called 'Spice', go on a hunt for a new manager, and manage to engage the experienced impresario, Simon Fuller. With his endorsement and negotiating power, they sign with Virgin Records. They go to the Brit Awards in 1996 where word is going round that Virgin has a new band, which everyone refers to as 'those Spice *girls*', so they change the name accordingly. In July 1996 'Wannabe' comes out as a single, and goes to number one for seven weeks.

In *Top of the Pops* magazine the editor, Peter Lorraine, has the idea of illustrating a feature on the band with five spice jars and the girls' heads, and he invents a nickname for each of them: Ginger, Scary, Sporty, Baby and Posh. By November that year, they are turning on the Oxford Street Christmas lights. At the next Brit Awards, in 1997, they have a bestselling album and are headlining at the event, for which Geri Halliwell (now 'Ginger Spice') spontaneously improvises a cheeky and soon-to-be-iconic Union Jack mini-dress.

The stratospheric rise to fame of the Spice Girls already demonstrates a pattern, which I shall argue is typical: it's a complex sequence of planned and unplanned events, a constantly evolving pattern of gestures and responses. The Herberts started with an intention to create a band, but the band that eventually emerged from the individuals they had brought together eluded their control, and created itself and its repertoire. Yet however attractive the Spice Girls' initial offering might have been, the chances are it would never have achieved mass popularity without a publicity machine of the sort led by Simon Fuller. And certain specific elements that turn out to be most important to their long term success appear at first as fortuitous and unexpected: the distinctive nicknames, the Union Jack dress.

But at this point in the story, Victoria's fame was barely beginning – and in her book she admits '*I* always wanted to be more famous than Persil Automatic', not *we*. The way her personal fame would continue to evolve throughout the following years and decades would be inextricably linked with the fame of a young footballer she fell in love with and married. All five Spice Girls have actively maintained a degree of celebrity since the break-up of the original group, but arguably Victoria's fame always kept the greatest momentum, and it's hard not to attribute this in part to her marriage.

When they met, David Beckham was a rising star at Manchester United, which itself was at that time well on its way to becoming the most famous football club in the world and a global superbrand. He was known for a particularly elegant and creative style of football, and for his impossibly good looks – he otherwise came across as agreeably modest, even shy to the point of inarticulacy. Yet, behind this boy-next-door persona, he had also from the beginning of his career taken an extremely businesslike approach to the management of his fame and fortune. At the age of 16, when not yet even playing for the Manchester United first team, he appointed as his agent Tony Spencer, who represented football's biggest stars of the day like Alan Shearer. Spencer would ensure, over the following years, that as Beckham's career developed he had a constant series of sponsorship and advertising deals, which both enhanced his personal fame, and made money out of it. At the time he first met Victoria (he was 24, she was 25), David was about to sign a £4m promotional deal with Brylcreem, and he was already as experienced at playing the fame game as she was.

There is no reason to suspect that David and Victoria's mutual attraction was other than spontaneous and genuine. (Although, ironically, it was Simon Fuller who first introduced them, he absolutely did not want Victoria Adams to be seen with David Beckham – his script for the Spice Girls at that time didn't include boyfriends, least of all famous footballers.) Yet their alliance has had a long lasting beneficial effect on both their careers as celebrities, and they have jointly managed this process with skill , energy, and the best professional help – though the Spice Girls fired Simon Fuller in 1998, finding him too controlling, David would hire him a few years later to replace Spencer as his agent, and since then Fuller has worked closely with both Beckhams in their various enterprises.

Yet what does it mean to say that the Beckhams have 'managed their fame'? At one extreme – the 'essentialist' view – it suggests that everything has been carefully calculated from the start – that the move of both from their respective starting careers towards the world of fashion, the naming of their children, every change of haircut or outfit, David's moves from one football club to another, Victoria's choice of musical genres, have all been part of some grand plan in which the couple judge all their actions by a consistent scheme of Beckham 'brand values' or 'personality'. At the other extreme, it could mean that their energy and popular appeal comes from being spontaneous, doing what they really want to do, and taking risks, and the only thing they really have needed to pay attention to is using their energy, activity, and fame to create more fame – fame, like money, being a currency that enables them to do more of what they enjoy doing.

Of course, we can never really know how the Beckhams manage their business and their lives on a daily basis. And even their own published accounts of what they do are themselves part of a publicity process, which may be engineered rather than entirely transparent. Nevertheless, based on what accounts I've seen, I strongly suspect that the basic process of managing 'brand Beckham' is much closer to the 'spontaneous/ responsive' end of the spectrum than then 'values-driven/ prescriptive' end.

Let's consider one micro-example, a long time ago now but still widely remembered: the episode of David's sarong. Here's an account from a book written in 2004 by Andy Milligan, then of the Interbrand brand consultancy. He starts from the assumption that the Beckham brand has always been prescriptively managed, using a version of the essentialist brand model:

> Not long before the 1998 World Cup, Beckham shocked the footballing world by turning up at a restaurant in a sarong… Beckham seemed to be *consciously setting a different agenda for himself and for footballers in general. With Posh's support*, he was clearly making his sense of style *an integral part of his brand identity.*

> This was a *smart move in PR terms.* He was making the most of his looks and encouraging fashion houses to consider him not just as a footballer but as a style icon. [p.96, *emphasis added*]

Compare that with Victoria's version, from *Learning to Fly*:

> …David had been out shopping with Jimmy Gulzar a couple of weeks before and they had both bought these Jean Paul Gaultier sarongs. It was totally David's idea. He wore one because he liked the look. We were just going out to dinner one night and he decided to wear it, just wrapped over a pair of trousers – I mean at resorts in Bali men wear them all the time. He's never worn one since, and who can blame him after all the flak he gets. But this was a summer night in Èze on the French Riviera – what did they expect him to wear? A three piece suit or football strip? (p. 202)

Is this disingenuous? Does the lady perhaps protest a bit too much? Perhaps the 'truth', if there is such a thing, lies somewhere between the two accounts. Certainly, the sarong episode suggests a man distinctly less macho and more at ease with his own masculinity than some popular stereotypes of the British footballer, and it did contribute to Beckham's subsequent reputation as a fashion leader with his own individuality. Yet I find it easier to believe that this originated more as a spontaneous bit of fun on a summer's evening than as a calculated strategy. And Victoria is adamant here, as elsewhere in the book, that she has very little influence over what David wears.

Does this matter? In terms of the outcome, probably not. A gesture need not have any conscious intention at all; even if it does, what it communicates to an observer is often very different from what is intended. If I look at my watch while you are talking to me, you may interpret this as me being short of time, or you being boring, or me being rude, when if anything I was checking how much time we had left for our conversation. As Paul Watzlawick has observed, it is impossible not to communicate, even if we have no intention to communicate anything at all by what we do; we are meaning-making creatures, with a strong compulsion to make sense of what might otherwise appear random behaviours. So the intention behind David Beckham's action that evening is irrelevant to its outcome. Its meaning, or more accurately its meanings, were determined by the multiple ways in which others responded to it. Some may have thought he looked a fool or effeminate, others may have thought he looked cool and sexy, some thought it was a self-serving stunt, some thought it was all Posh's idea, some just thought he was having fun, so those are all part of what it 'meant'.

The managers of both brands and celebrities often aim for a high degree of control over what happens. They worry that this is 'on-brand' or 'off-brand', this 'wouldn't fit your image', that 'isn't true to our brand values', or it would have some negative connotation. For instance, Victoria recalls that one of the band's stylists tried hard to stop Geri wearing that Union Jack dress at the 1997 Brit Awards, terrified they'd be seen as National Front.

Yet fame is constructed out of the cumulative effects of all the actors' individual choices and gestures. Some of these will be co-ordinated or planned, but very often the ones that turn out to matter most won't, and can't be – perhaps because those which exhibit spontaneity, energy, unexpectedness, ambiguity, and individuality, rather than trying too cautiously to follow a script, are those which stimulate the most lively responses.

The sarong is not an isolated example of the potential gap between the celebrity gesture and the public response. Let's take another: when David Beckham in 1999 swapped his floppy, Brylcreem'd locks for a shaven head, responses were legion. Some saw it as a penitential response to his disastrous sending off in the 1998 World Cup game against Argentina, for which he had been vilified in the press. Andy Milligan again offers his own interpretations:

> … a serious shaved haircut that signalled his intention to do the business on the pitch… in addition, it marked his rite of passage from single man to husband and father.

These sound plausible, and may well have been among the ways people made sense of Beckham's new 'do' . But here, too, the account in Victoria's memoir suggests none of these meanings may have been intended:

> It was Tyler [Victoria's own hair stylist] who said David should have all his hair cut off in the spring. David would have been happy with just a bit of a crop.
>
> 'It's all or nothing', Tyler had said. And David trusted Tyler enough to agree (p.328).

Perhaps the most important thing we can say with confidence about David's change of hairstyle (there would be many more) is that it got him noticed anew and talked about. It kept him in the news and created a buzz. It was powerful precisely because it was an ambiguous gesture which stimulated people to make their own interpretations.

If we can generalise from these small examples, we could at least suggest that in order to maintain fame over time – to be sufficiently interesting to the media and to the public – unexpected novelty is often much more powerful than consistency. Yet the essentialist view of brands tends to prize consistency over anything else, and generally sees change as a source of risk.

*

But let's take a step back. Every day, millions of men change their hairstyles and decide what to wear when they go out, and nobody outside their immediate circle notices or cares. What were the circumstances that made David Beckham's apparently trivial actions into matters of concern and interest and apparent significance to millions of people?

David Beckham was (is) a supremely talented footballer, and good looking into the bargain. Without these intrinsic skills and attributes, there's no reason to assume he would have ever been heard of outside his own circle of friends and acquaintances (though it's always a possibility in some parallel universe). But there are thousands of talented footballers and good looking guys around the world who can go out to dinner without their outfits becoming front page news. What got David Beckham into this position was not his intrinsic qualities alone, but a long series of events, some planned and some unplanned (and some perhaps forever ambiguous), which built his fame to a point where this degree of media interest became inevitable.

It must have made a difference, for instance, that from an early age he was signed with Manchester United, who during that period were becoming the most famous team in the world. And the club's fame, in its turn, was made possible by the growth and dominance of the Premier League as a global phenomenon. It's hard to imagine (though again, not impossible) that David Beckham would have become as famous as he did if he'd only ever played for Preston North End.

The choice of team may or may not have been part of a grand plan, but David's decision to engage Tony Spencer as his agent from a very early age was. As a result, he had a series of promotional contracts which, as well as generating a lot of money, ensured his face and name became familiar to mass audiences, in the UK and elsewhere.

By the time he met Victoria, he was already sufficiently famous that their connection made instant news: *Learning to Fly* has several stories, both funny and rather sad, about their early efforts to meet without attracting press attention. As the story broke, it multiplied the media coverage for both of them (even though, as already mentioned, Simon Fuller tried to discourage their relationship).

Another key event was, we can only assume, unplanned: David's sending off at the 1998 World Cup after he was seen to aim a petulant and rather pointless kick at an opponent. England, a man down, went on to lose the game. For a while he went from Hero to Zero, and was vilified by the media. Yet it also provided a compelling storyline from the point of view of building fame, an episode that people could and did enjoy arguing and pontificating about, which revealed him as a more complicated, more human character, which invited sympathy as well as condemnation. And it set up a completely new context for whatever happened next, so that when, for example, he appeared with a shaved head, people were quick to read all kinds of meanings into his action which wouldn't have been there before.

These are only a few points from a much longer and more complex story, but they may be enough to suggest some of the conditions that make fame possible. I'll outline these briefly now, but will return to them as we go on to develop them as a tentative template for how we could think about the creation of fame, whether for brands, celebrities, or anything else.

1. Some intrinsic qualities are needed which will be compelling or attractive enough for the celebrity to appeal to the public and, first of all, gain admittance to a platform from which the public can be appealed to.

2. But what is also needed is the ability to access audiences repeatedly and on a massive scale. It is very rare for this to happen automatically as a

result of intrinsic talent: some mechanism for achieving mass exposure must also be employed. In the case of the Beckhams, this ability to command mass exposure was initially contrived by their agents (Fuller and Spencer), access to events or contexts that already had mass audiences (the Brits, Virgin Records, Manchester United), and soon by themselves becoming a news story which media could not resist covering.

3. The celebrity must be associated with enough unique and memorable images or other 'distinctive assets' to be immediately recognisable and distinctive. Their distinctive assets, besides their faces, included nicknames and jokes ('Posh and Becks', Beckingham Palace), hairstyles and outfits.

4. When the combination of intrinsic qualities, distinctive assets and mass exposure reach a certain critical point, social diffusion kicks in and multiplies the effects: this is driven both by the public and the media in a symbiotic relationship. Social diffusion is often powerfully enhanced by controversy or ambiguity, as press and public alike respond to events by trying to make sense of them or arguing about them.

The management of fame therefore involves three territories beside the most obvious one of ensuring that the intrinsic appeal of the brand/celebrity/ product is maintained. There must be a conscious strategy for reaching mass audiences (repeatedly); careful nurturing of distinctive assets; and the use of the many techniques which exist for enabling and encouraging social diffusion.

None of this is very new. The formula describes Barnum's success with Jenny Lind (or indeed the Feejee Mermaid). Jenny Lind was, as the *Times* put it, merely 'a talented vocalist'. Her talent as a performer had already made her famous enough in Europe to attract Barnum's attention. But it was Barnum who created the platform for her to perform, and attracted the mass audiences who would become aware of her (by no means limited only to those wealthy enough to actually hear her perform), by providing news stories which the media of the day were keen to present to their mass audiences. He published visual images and stories about Jenny through a wide variety of channels (including merchandise) which both enhanced her distinctiveness and made her more interesting and appealing to the public – and they, and the media, responded to all this by writing and talking about her, in ways both adulatory and critical. The important thing was that she continued to make news. (And after she parted company with Barnum and changed her name, she made much less news, though Barnum continued to build his own fame until the end of his life by using the same techniques.)

I do not think that the success of the Beckhams is either random or artless. They both set out to be famous, and have succeeded as a result of their hard work and extraordinary energy. There is clearly much conscious intention and active planning involved, as from the outset both David and Victoria have been canny enough to consciously manage their fame and engage the best people to help them do so (and ruthlessly to change advisers too, when they chose to). The significantly named Beckham Brand Holdings continues to post multi-million pound revenues and profits – the couple have always run their lives as a highly successful commercial enterprise.

But neither do I think the whole programme is planned or prescriptive. Their fame continues to emerge from the interaction of their own spontaneity and personal choices, unplanned or unexpected events, and the ways in which they choose to respond to these.

To put it another way, the whole saga can easily be conceived of as a performance – not a performance scripted from beginning to end, but a continually improvised performance in which every interaction, audience response, and chance happening (even mistakes) can be utilised for the overriding purpose of keeping the audience in their seats and enjoying the show.

I will continue to analyse fame by looking on it as an outcome of the four dimensions of intrinsic appeal, mass exposure, distinctiveness, and social diffusion. But the crucial factor for success is what we might call a fame mindset. The fame mindset is energetic and fearless, responsive and improvisatory more than it is cautious and controlling. It is not without intelligence, nor lacking in strategy, but it must also trust its own judgment and intuition, it must be prepared to seize opportunities without hesitation and, frequently, to take risks. It must not only endure controversy, misunderstanding, and even the most aggressive attacks, but must know how to turn these, ju-jitsu like, to its own advantage.

These are all qualities which we can observe throughout the career of Barnum, and they are also to be recognised in the history of most successful brands. There are some obvious differences between brands and celebrities – celebrities are ultimately real individuals with a tangible existence, however much they may succeed in projecting an 'image', while brands are abstractions representing what may be very loose and variable collections of goods and services. So you might suppose that while human celebrities can flourish on spontaneity, unpredictability, and change, a non-human brand can, and maybe should, be subject to much more rigorous planning and control.

Yet the histories of the great brands repeatedly show a similar pattern of emergence and evolution, of improvisatory responses to unexpected events, where confidence and energy, responsiveness, and the ability to create continual interest and attractiveness, are more important than adherence to abstract ideas of consistency. As an example of what I mean, let's move on from the Beckhams to look into the history of a classic, global brand – one which is perhaps in many people's minds the archetype of 'branding' – Coca-Cola.

Chapter Seven

Energy, Essence and Icons

B ut before I begin to tell something of the story of Coca-Cola, I have a confession to make.

I have said some critical things about what I call the 'essentialist' view of brands, and I expect to say more. Yet for a considerable period I actively developed and taught this way of thinking throughout the worldwide agency network I then worked for.

It was the mid-nineties, and already we at DDB were rather late to the party. Somewhere around 1990, the expression 'brand equity' had suddenly become the great marketing buzzword. Since the fifties there had been talk of 'brand image' or 'brand personality', but many clients saw these as rather lightweight concepts, ad agency jargon that had little to do with sales or profits.

Then in the 1980s a spate of mergers and acquisitions raised again the slightly forgotten question of what brands were actually worth. The official accountancy position was that as 'intangible assets' they weren't really worth anything, so although one company might in practice pay a lot to buy a famous brand, they could not include what they'd paid for as an asset on their balance sheet. Into this anomalous situation stepped a bright young entrepreneur called John Murphy.

Murphy had set up a small consultancy offering brand naming services, which he eventually called Interbrand. He now invented (literally one weekend, across his kitchen table) a methodology for valuing brands in a way that was relatively replicable and transparent – and therefore acceptable to accountants. One rapid effect of this was to remind brand owners of the simple truth that John Stuart had passed on years before at the lunch table, that brands could be worth massive sums of money. In the eighties of Gordon Gecko and Wall Street, the inspired coining of 'brand equity' quickly took over from the illusory-sounding 'brand image'.

So we at DDB, like most other agencies and consultants, were looking – belatedly – to climb on the brand equity bandwagon. Other agencies, notably Y&R, had already created what were known as 'brand equity monitors' – huge scale, multi-category global consumer surveys that set out to measure degrees of popular attachment to a long list of brands. Y&R had successfully used their survey, the Brand Asset Valuator (BAV) to attract clients and prospects, so we wanted one too; though we only had a fraction of Y&R's budget, my colleagues in Chicago, experienced quantitative researchers, produced our version, which we called Brand Capital. (This kind of research, incidentally, is completely different from Interbrand-style financial valuations, which classically don't use any consumer research at all.)

But the project I was more personally involved in was creating what was generically known as a Brand Equity Model. As marketing theory now re-focused on the idea that brands were valuable assets, brand owners naturally began to pose the question: how then do we nurture and grow such assets? There was no existing formula or process in place, but over the years a bewildering number of concepts related to brands had grown up that seemed potentially relevant: *brand loyalty, brand positioning* (invented around 1970 by ex-admen Al Ries and Jack Trout), *brand awareness*, the established language of *brand image* and *brand personality* (originated by Gardner and Levy in 1955), old advertising ideas like *consumer benefits* (functional or emotional) and even *'reasons why'*, other standard marketing tropes like *target markets*, and organisational consultants' notions of *'supra-ordinate goals'* or *higher purpose*, all came into the mix.

Brand Equity models aimed to clarify and organise this conceptual muddle, a task which most of them approached by trying to include as many different elements as possible (and thereby generally avoiding having to make any hard choices between them). Academics, consultants, ad agencies and even brand owners themselves all came up with their different versions. Most of these used some kind of geometric or pictorial device to organise their complicated material in an apparently coherent way – Jean-Noel Kapferer, a French academic, came up with a deeply philosophical six-sided 'prism', the American Kevin Lane Keller later produced a pyramid, and Unilever had a proprietary 'Brand Key' shaped like a keyhole, while others, not always credited, put about ' brand temples' (with foundations, pillars, and a pediment), and the notorious yet perennially popular 'brand onion', many different versions of which can still be found by a quick Google search.

It is perhaps no coincidence that this was the age when PowerPoint graphics were still new enough to be exciting, and many people quickly discovered that a set of concentric circles or a triangle or a star or a lot of arrows were a marvellous way to create an illusion of connectedness without being at all clear about what, if anything, these might actually mean.

Anyway, I admit, we did all this too. I worked principally with a brilliant French colleague who had previously worked with Kapferer and we hammered out our own model, which we called Brand Foundations™. We could not deny it bore a family resemblance to most of the other versions that were around, though we liked to believe ours was the best of the bunch, and in truth, it wasn't bad. You had to imagine the brand (a quasi-person) asking itself a series of introspective questions, the answers to which were expected to be decisive, directional, and inspiring:

1.   Where do I come from? (Origins and History)

2.   What do I do? (Field of Competence)

3.   What makes me different? (Point of Difference)

4.   Who am I for? (The Imagined Customer)

5. What am I like as a person? (Personality)

6. What do I fight for? (The Fight)

7. What do I value? (The Value)

8. Strategic Concept ('Can we summarise the central idea of the Brand Foundations in one short phrase…?')

Initially this didn't have any visualisation, but it wasn't long before I sat down with PowerPoint one day and made a lovely flower with seven petals and a centre which we all used thereafter.

I wrote all this up in some detail as a training manual for our entire network, and for several, mostly very enjoyable years, I travelled the world initiating our staff into how to use the tool. There was much about it that was attractive and apparently useful: it forced our clients, and ourselves, to ask some searching and often productive questions about the brand. We had a lot of bright people who were capable of using the questions in creative and generative ways, and Brand Foundations sessions and interviews, however they were organised, could feel like positive and stimulating experiences.

But I also slowly became aware of two other phenomena – not limited to our brand model, but equally true of others I had to work with when clients chose other consultants to lead the process. One was the moment, which nearly always happened, when an energetic and creative conversation about the brand's history or meaning or purpose morphed into a soul-destroying argument about the niceties of language, as we tried to agree some formal answers to the questions and so 'conclude' the process. As this kind of word-smithing dragged on, you could feel the energy almost literally draining out of the group, and by the end most people were ready to agree to anything to get out of the meeting room. The other interesting moment was when you presented the answers, the finely-tuned verbal outcome of what had usually been a lengthy process, to anyone who had not been part of it so far. Suddenly the formula that you had sweated and argued over (something like, 'we exist to bring people together') was met with initial apathy, often closely followed by antagonism.

Because of these limitations, Brand Foundations™ – though it always felt it should have such potential – somehow never quite delivered the results in the real world that it promised. If it did have a positive effect (and of a sort that is hard to measure) it was as a result of senior people spending time together, having a generative conversation that they would not otherwise have had. The formal output, however, remained an inert and unhelpful piece of paper, at worst inhibiting action rather than stimulating it.

The reason I insert this apparent digression at this point – while you are still waiting to hear about Coca-Cola – is that in my Brand Foundations training sessions I almost invariably chose Coke as a brand for the group to practise on. Because of its global familiarity and its rich and comparatively well-known history, just about everyone felt capable of having a view about it. The sessions were, indeed, nearly always stimulating and even fun; presented with the list of questions, people easily found lots to talk about and argue about. We never, as you might suspect, came to any agreed let alone definitive answers, but in a training session it was easy to defer that to another day. If people were asked what was Coke's 'core value', for example, many possibilities would be offered: *refreshment, togetherness, fun, family, America, global harmony, stimulation, authenticity…* you can easily continue the list yourself, and you can also see, with a moment's thought, that any one of these words (or your own attempt) seems plausible because it relates to some specific skeins of the brand's rich and complex history. But it is not clear what would be gained by privileging any one of them over the others.

It also seems doubtful to me whether Coca-Cola, in reality, at any stage of its development, has owed its growth and success to finding clear answers to these kind of questions. Even while I was using Coke as my guinea-pig brand for Brand Foundations training, I was already familiar with Mark Pendergrast's authoritative history, *For God, Country and Coca-Cola*. For some reason I never consciously related the two. Yet it now seems to me obvious that simply reviewing the historical sequence of events that led to Coca-Cola achieving and maintaining its global dominance as a brand should be enough to demonstrate that brands do not grow out of 'brand essences', however cleverly devised, but out of something very different.

Pendergrast's book is a thick volume, though never less than fascinating.

Like any good history, it reminds us that reality is messy and complicated, events never entirely predictable. Any brief summary therefore will be a gross oversimplification. So I will restrict my focus in this chapter to two episodes:

+ the first three decades of the brand, encompassing its spectacular growth up to about the First World War;

+ its adoption during the Second World War as a symbol of America throughout the world.

In the following chapter, I will look at the genesis of one specific Coca-Cola commercial, the 1971 'Hilltop', and discuss its consequences for the brand and business. (And no, it wasn't written by Don Draper; the real story is much more interesting.)

But first, back to the beginning.

Episode 1: How Coca-Cola 'became a go' – why energy matters more than essence

The phenomenal growth of Coca-Cola sales up to the time of the Great War was largely due to the talents and efforts of three men.

Dr John Pemberton, an Atlanta chemist, developed the formula in 1885, a powerful combination of coca nuts (a natural source of cocaine) and stimulating cola leaves, with some syrup and herbal flavours to make it palatable. Pemberton was already successfully marketing a mixture of similar ingredients with wine as 'Vin Coca' (itself an imitation of another brand, 'Vin Mariani'), but anticipating that Atlanta would soon vote to ban alcohol, as it did in 1885, he saw an opportunity for a 'temperance' alternative. Though the formula had much in common with many of the patent medicines that were then strongly advertised, Pemberton envisaged his tonic from the outset being delivered in the form of a carbonated beverage, as all that was needed was to mix the base syrup with soda at any of the 'soda fountains' that were then ubiquitous in Atlanta's torrid climate.

However, Pemberton, a morphine addict and in failing health, would never have achieved more than a fleeting success with his new drink without the contributions of two other men. His loyal assistant, Frank Robinson, not only manufactured the product but wrote the advertisements and took charge of the publicity, clearly positioning it in its early years as an 'intellectual beverage and temperance drink'. Perhaps of the greatest long term significance for the brand, it was Robinson whose copper-plate handwriting formed the 'script' logo which is still familiar today.

But the man who drove the sales of Coca-Cola far beyond Atlanta and all expectations was the entrepreneur Asa G. Candler, who bought the rights to the drink from Pemberton shortly before the inventor's death in 1888 (in circumstances which are complicated, obscure, and apparently rather dodgy). Candler's driving forces were unlimited ambition and confidence, and – with the continuing loyal support of Frank Robinson – he worked untiringly to expand the drink's distribution and invested increasingly in promoting it. Point of purchase signs, calendars, novelty merchandise and newspaper ads all prominently displayed the Coca-Cola script. Initially the advertising focused mainly on medicinal claims, but as sales grew exponentially through the 1890s Frank Robinson realised this was holding back the drink's potential – so from this point on the ads focused more on the simple claim 'Drink Coca-Cola. Delicious and Refreshing.' As ad budgets increased proportionate to sales, newspaper ads were joined by streetcar signs, serving trays, thermometers, clocks, pencils, bookmarks, and calendars featuring attractive young women and celebrities. By 1900 Robinson was sending out over a million promotional items a year.

About this time the business took another leap forward: Candler was belatedly persuaded to allow third party contracts to sell the drink ready mixed in bottles, thus expanding its availability beyond the limits of the soda fountain. (The casual terms in these contracts would cause huge problems for the company in decades to come.) By 1912 advertising expenditure exceeded a million dollars a year, making Coke the most advertised brand in the United States. In a way that may by now begin to feel familiar, the brand passed into popular culture: Betty, the 1914 calendar girl, became a national sensation, and the brand appeared in songs, moving pictures, and (to Candler's dismay) a notorious sex scandal involving the film star Fatty Arbuckle. (Don't ask.)

Coca-Cola had long been more than a national success – it was a phenomenon. But one of the penalties for the drink's fame was the huge number of unlicensed imitators it attracted, under names like Cafe-Coca, Coke-Ola, Cola Coke, Coca and Cola, Kola-Kola, and so on (Pendergrast lists over eighty, and that wasn't even all of them). Fortuitously, Asa Candler's brother, John, ran a top law practice, and from 1904 onwards he dedicated one of his brightest young lawyers, Harold Hirsch, to the full time job of protecting the Coca-Cola trademark. Hirsch, supported by the strengthened U.S. Trademark Law of 1905, made it his life's mission to pursue and prosecute trademark infringements with all the zeal of a medieval witch finder. By 1926, it's estimated he had won over 7,000 such cases, and a fat three-volume 'Bible' of Coca-Cola law was widely circulated to intimidate anyone who was rash enough to try it on.

To create a demand and then allow others to satisfy it was known in the early years of the twentieth century as 'the problem of substitution'. Claude Hopkins wrote about it:

> Many pioneers in a line establish large demands, then, through some fault in their foundations, lose a large share of it in the harvest. Theirs is a *mere brand*, for instance, where it might have stood for an exclusive product.

> Vaseline is an example. That product established a new demand, then almost monopolized that demand through wisdom at the start. To have called it *some brand of petroleum jelly* might have made a difference of millions in results. (1923, *emphasis added*)

Hopkins hardly ever uses the word *brand*, and the way he uses it here begins to explain why: a 'mere brand' describes a highly substitutable product that just happens to carry a name without particular significance. The use of the word brand, to mean 'just a name', and the contrast with 'exclusive product', is almost the opposite of the way we tend to talk today. What is clear is that Hopkins is fully aware of the importance of creating specific demand for a trademark that will be resistant to 'substitution'.

So was Harold Hirsch, and defending the trademark in the courts was only one way of doing this. He also realised that the design of the bottle could play an important part. As more and more of the drink was sold ready bottled, Hirsch urged the bottlers in 1914 to see beyond the short term expense of creating a distinctive bottle design, and made his long term view of the business explicit:

> We are not building Coca-Cola alone for today. We are building Coca-Cola forever, and it is our hope that Coca-Cola will remain the National drink to the end of time.

The company invited various glass works to propose some prototypes. In Terre Haute, Indiana, an employee of the Root Glass Company was sent to the public library to find inspiration in pictures of the drink's ingredients. Unable to find any suitable visuals of either the coca leaf or kola nut, he came away instead with a picture of a cocoa bean, maybe even confusing cocoa with coca. Its fluted and curved shape would become the first version of the iconic Coca-Cola bottle that we still recognise today.

The highly distinctive Coke bottle has since become loaded with different meanings; from the very start, when it was known as the 'hobbleskirt' bottle, many people saw it as 'feminine'. Yet none of this was in the mind of Harold Hirsch, nor of the designers who created it. Hirsch wanted it only to be distinctive and impossible to copy, while the designer was following the inspiration of something that turned out to be entirely unrelated and fortuitous – a cocoa bean.

This story so far shows clearly that the growth of Coca-Cola was not random or fortuitous; it was the outcome of a consistent and ruthlessly applied business strategy, whose three main principles could be easily summed up as

- continually extend physical availability

- invest heavily in advertising and publicity of all kinds

- aggressively protect trademarks.

But apart from this, there is little evidence of consistency, nor of a consistent 'vision' for the brand. Trademarks began as comparatively random gestures (the script logo, the bottle design), the 'positioning' shifted from medicinal to refreshment without ever entirely abandoning the first, target audiences were continually added to (women, smokers, children, office workers, families...), and advertising used multiple themes – ranging from claims about the effects of the product to an extensive use of pretty girls and celebrity endorsements, repeating simple slogans that became associated with Coke but were otherwise fairly undifferentiated ('delicious and refreshing'), and often simply 'keeping the name before the public' on walls, bar tops, clocks, matchbooks, calendars, and a hundred and one other bits of merchandise. Even the product itself underwent an important change: in 1901 Candler, in response to increasingly damaging criticism of the syrup's ingredients, quietly removed any traces of cocaine, subsequently denying that it had ever been part of the formula.

In other words, there was never a 'single compelling idea' or 'proposition' behind the brand, it had no 'DNA' or 'essence', and it had no 'higher purpose' – unless we accept the quasi-religious belief in the product's benefits with which Asa Candler and his colleagues indoctrinated their workforce.

What drove its success was much less mystical. As one of Pemberton's relatives remarked somewhat ruefully long after the inventor's death,

> Coca-Cola became a go because it was pushed and pushed by an energetic man. If the Pembertons had not sold the formula it probably would have stayed in an old drink somewhere and been lost in time.

But of course, the story of how Coca-Cola 'became a go' is entirely consistent with the theories of Byron Sharp and the Ehrenberg-Bass institute: the brand continually attracted more and more users through a combination of building physical availability and mental availability, supported by rigorous management of its distinctive assets. It built an ever more complex network of associations linking the brand with a wide range of occasions, benefits, target audiences, and attractive images from popular culture. Far from being based on a 'single minded idea', the spectacular levels of mental availability achieved by Coca-Cola were fuelled by the endless variety of its manifestations and meanings, from brain tonic to refreshing drink, from sexy film stars to painted wall signs at gas stations. The consistency lay only (but crucially) in its adherence to its distinctive assets

– the script logo, the classic bottle, the colour scheme, the name – all of which company lawyers fought tirelessly to protect.

But, you may object, all this is early history, primitive stuff. Since then Coca-Cola has become an image charged with meaning, a global 'cultural icon'. Surely there is more to this than merely 'keeping your name before the public'? Well, perhaps.

Episode 2: How Coca-Cola won the War – The Limits of 'Cultural Branding'

Asa Candler was succeeded by his son Howard, but the younger man lacked his father's ruthless drive and in 1922 the Syndicate which now owned the company replaced him with 33-year-old Robert Woodruff. Woodruff had all Asa Candler's energy and ambition, and was arguably more organised and a better leader: he would preside over Coca-Cola's continued growth for the next sixty years. Woodruff standardised and systematised all aspects of the business, improving quality and reliability. Having already got Coke into every grocery store and soda fountain in the USA, he pushed for ever more outlets such as filling stations, his strategy being that the drink should always be 'within an arm's reach of desire'. Publicity was driven by his contemporary Archie Lee of the D'Arcy ad agency, who came up with the slogans 'Thirst knows no season', and then, 'The pause that refreshes', which shaped much of the brand's advertising for more than two decades – though they never really dropped the earlier 'Delicious and Refreshing'.

Under Lee, adverts became less wordy and more visual, employing famous artists such as Norman Rockwell to create emotional images of rural innocence, peaceful harmony, bustling cityscapes and of course the perennial pretty girls. In 1931 the illustrator Haddon Sundblom created an image of Santa Claus which would forever identify him as a fat jolly man dressed in Coke scarlet and white. Sales continued to grow, and Coca-Cola was one of very few stocks that lost no value in the 1929 stockmarket crash. Many predicted disaster for the drink when prohibition was repealed in 1933, but this didn't happen either. Throughout the Roaring Twenties and the Great Depression of the Thirties, Coca-Cola became an increasingly ubiquitous part of American life, promoting images which symbolised values of pleasure, relaxation, and refreshment regardless of whatever else was going on in the world.

Soon after the attack on Pearl Harbor which brought America into the war,

> Robert Woodruff issued an extraordinary order: 'We will see that every man in uniform gets a bottle of Coca-Cola for five cents, wherever he is and whatever it costs our company'. Woodruff's gesture was undoubtedly a genuine act of patriotism, but his shrewd business sense and eye for publicity also prompted his magnanimity (p.199).

Within the USA itself, the war years were not easy for Coca-Cola sales – the company was hampered by sugar rationing and hard pressed by a revived Pepsi-Cola who offered a larger bottle at a lower price. But in the longer term Woodruff's bold move both consolidated Coke's already established image at home as America's national beverage, and established the basis for a global demand which had so far remained largely unexploited. The title of Pendergrast's book, *For God, Country, and Coca-Cola*, accurately reflects the powerful combination of emotional meanings which the brand carried for millions of G.I.s posted far from home, a mixture of happy memories, patriotism, and a quasi-religious sense of comfort and security.

For one recent theorist of branding, Woodruff's bold move during the war was more than an inspired way to maximise an opportunity: it represents the point at which Coca-Cola changed from being a mere brand to becoming an 'iconic brand'. According to Douglas Holt, everything Coke had done up to this point was what he disparagingly calls 'mind-share techniques' – 'but beginning with its innovative use of advertising and public relations during World War II, Coke was soon transformed into a powerful iconic brand'.

What does this mean? Holt begins his book with the OED definition of cultural icon, as 'a person or thing regarded as a representative symbol, especially of a culture or movement'. (Currently Wikipedia offers a similar definition, 'A cultural icon is an artefact that is identified by members of a culture as representative of that culture.') It's true that Coca-Cola has for a long time fitted this definition as a 'representative symbol' of American culture. But while the Second World War proved a great opportunity to strengthen this symbolism and spread it far beyond the USA itself, Coca-Cola as a symbol of America long pre-dates Pearl Harbor. Its status as America's 'National drink', already recognised as a fact by Harold Hirsch in 1914, had been gradually developed over many decades through a relentless programme of ubiquity, experiences of the brand in connection to all aspects of American daily life, and advertising which, especially from Archie Lee's time onward, presented a wide range of idealised images of 'the American way of life'.

Had this not already been the case, it is unlikely that any grand gesture on Woodruff's part would have turned the brand into a national symbol. Many other brands, in the US and UK, used the war to wrap themselves in the national flag (as others had in the Great War, or even in the Boer War) – mostly they were regarded as suspect for doing so. Woodruff's wartime strategy only worked as it did because it reflected an existing reality for millions of G.I.s. (And their Generals too – Eisenhower was a particular devotee of Coca-Cola.)

So we could justifiably call Coca-Cola a 'cultural icon'. But this status was something that had already emerged over time as a by-product of something much more fundamentally important – the brand's fame, its mental and physical availability, and its rich mental associative network, all of which had been built, over many decades, by managers with those qualities of 'energy and ingenuity' which P.T. Barnum had boasted were the secret of success.

What Holt calls 'cultural branding' has enough truth in it to sound plausible; things that want to stay famous need to be responsive to changing times, attitudes, and fashions, and occasionally they do something that so captures a popular mood or moment in time that it has a greater than usual impact. Holt, and his later collaborator Doug Cameron, are splendidly (and I think justifiably) rude about what they call the 'brand bureaucracy' of brand essences and brand onions. But while their books are well worth reading (and you can make up your own mind), for me their dismissal of 'mind-share' ignores the fundamental importance of fame creation in brand building.

My first problem with 'cultural branding' is that it only focuses on a small part of the whole. However you create a 'cultural icon', it's only one element in the bigger task of creating fame, one type of gesture in a continuing performance. It constitutes only one of the four dimensions necessary for fame – intrinsic interest. Unless it reaches a mass audience, unless it is distinctively branded, and unless it generates social diffusion, it will count for little.

My second difficulty with accepting 'cultural branding' as a practical approach is that it seems to me to substitute a different kind of essentialism for the brand bureaucracy Holt and Cameron so reject. It's much easier to post-rationalise the abstract meanings behind cultural phenomena than to start from abstract meanings and create something tangible. Of course, if you *can* make this approach work for you, that's great. But as Holt himself admits at the outset, the process of 'cultural branding' has in reality always been a tacit and emergent one:

> I've yet to find a cultural brand strategy articulated in formal documents like marketing plans, brand bibles, and creative briefs… cultural brand strategies have lurked primarily in the gut feel of ad agency creatives and other commercial artists. (p.xii)

It's not unreasonable to want to turn a tacit practice into an explicit one, but it's not always realistic; at worst, it leads only to another version of brand bureaucracy. As an alternative to trying to 'bureaucratise' a tacit process, we might consider instead what conditions allow such a tacit process to flourish, and which, conversely, block or inhibit it. A culture in which 'gut feel' is empowered and respected is one way of putting it. But we could add other ideas: a willingness to take risks, playfulness, subversiveness, an acceptance of physical pleasures, improvisation. All these are rather opposed to the cautious, intellectual approaches which are more usually dominant in organisations. That is not to say that one is right and one is wrong – there are good reasons for being cautious and for thinking about things – but there needs to be the right sort of balance, or perhaps dialectic, between the two.

When Geri Halliwell improvised her skimpy Union Jack dress for the Brit Awards, she added one more memorable image to the Spice Girls' stock. In the context of Thatcher's Britain it set up complex resonances of right-wing politics, women asserting political power ('girl power'), sexual dominance (as well as availability), and a carnival spirit of sending the whole thing up. Did Halliwell consciously think in these kinds of abstract concepts? I don't imagine she did. It's much more likely she was prompted by 'gut feel', or perhaps more accurately, an instinct for showmanship, for creating a gesture that she had a hunch would be ambiguous, intriguing, visually striking and above all controversial (as already mentioned, other members of the team tried hard to kill the dress, terrified they'd be identified as some kind of extreme right-wingers). When sociologists and semiologists and agency strategists try to analyse this sort of thing they are not entirely wrong: they are in their way paying tribute to the complex fascinations that such compelling gestures set up in the public. But they are not recreating in any sense the complex emergent and intuitive processes by which such gestures come into being.

Rather than attempt to bureaucratise the creative process, or, alternatively, to close down further discussion by using a phrase like 'creative gut-feel', we could choose instead to look in more detail at what actually happens when an 'iconic' gesture is created. And, to return to Coke, we are well placed to examine exactly how one particular 'cultural icon' of Coca-Cola came into being, because one of its creators wrote a whole book about it: the 1971 commercial that was known as 'Hilltop', and even better known as 'I'd like to teach the world to sing'.

Douglas Holt frames this commercial as a prime example of cultural branding, and a redemptive moment in the history of the brand:

> By the late 1960s... Coke's apple-pie celebrations of the American commonweal were wearing thin. Civil rights protests, a youth culture disenchanted with companies and middle-class life, and a very unpopular war in Vietnam were all tearing the country apart. Coke's suburban-nuclear myth had become naive, antiquated. Attempts to reconnect with consumers by means of a smorgasbord of tried-and-true Americana failed. (p.23)

Holt's cited source for this paragraph is Pendergrast's book, yet it's a very partial retelling of what Pendergrast actually wrote. It's true that the late sixties were in many ways a time of great 'cultural disruption', and also that the campaigns Coke ran in the mid sixties under the slogan 'Things go better with Coke' were relatively undistinguished – Pendergrast describes one commercial as 'flat, forced, and unbelievable'. Even so, there's no reason to believe that any of these ads were disastrous, or more damaging to the brand than not advertising would have been. But then, in 1969, Bill Backer of the McCann's agency resurrected an old slogan from 1942, 'It's the Real Thing'. With a new, catchy jingle, and films which combined traditional images of Americana with, for the first time, integrated scenes of black and white teenagers playing basketball, all combined with a major updating of the pack design, Coke, according to Pendergrast, had succeeded in getting back on track:

> Coca-Cola had miraculously implemented a slogan and campaign which appealed to both hawk and dove, National Guard and hippie, parent and child.

The following year, echoing the relaxed mood of popular hits of the time like 'Bridge Over Troubled Water' and 'Let It Be', Backer 'modified the "Real Thing" song as a quiet folk ballad, "Friendly Feelings" ...over visuals of happy, clean-cut young hippies....'. So, when 'Hilltop' followed a year later, it didn't come out of nowhere to transform a disastrous series of 'failed' ads; it grew out of a sequence of commercials which were already successful, it riffed off an existing end line, and built on existing themes of togetherness, serenity, youth and hope.

Yes, it's true that this film caught the mood of the times and seized the public's imagination. As Pendergrast puts it, 'The vision of the idealistic youths crooning to a weary world soothed like a hymn in an outdoor church....'. To that extent, it was great 'cultural branding'. But 'Hilltop' was not a radical departure from the commercials that had preceded it. It just happened to become more famous than the others. And the real story of how it came into being – as later written down in a full and thoughtful account by Bill Backer himself – is complex, fascinating, and sheds much light on how a successful creative process actually works in practice. As we shall see, the genesis of this commercial was fraught with disasters and crises, and makes the story of the Barclaycard campaign that began my book look like a walk in the park.

Chapter Eight

A Face in the Piazza Navona

W illiam Backer was born in 1926 and grew up in Charleston, South Carolina. He served in the US Navy in World War II and then went to Yale, where he studied music under the celebrated classical composer, Paul Hindemith. But his passion was always for popular music:

> ...during my years in the Navy and later on at Yale, I continually wrote songs and musical skits and shows – middle class, cozy, happy, very easy to sing and hard to forget. (p.24)

When Bill eventually found his way into advertising, at Young & Rubicam, it was no surprise that he approached selling as a branch of entertainment. Having written some radio commercials for Beech-Nut chewing gum, in 1958 he was able to persuade the client to sponsor an anarchic show for the newly named 'teenagers' which all other brands were running shy of. *The Dick Clark Saturday Night Beech-Nut Show* featured a procession of rising rock'n'roll stars who would appear for next to nothing to promote their own careers – Chuck Berry, Buddy Holly, Bill Haley, Jerry Lee Lewis, almost everyone except Elvis himself. As was then still common, the lines between content and promotion in the show were extremely blurred, with songs adapted to include mentions of the sponsor's product and commercials improvised live with groups of teenagers. It was very much the advertising world of *The Hucksters* and Beautee Soap ten years on, as it moved into the era of TV and rock'n'roll – and, just as singers had sold soap, Chuck Berry now sold chewing gum.

Moving on from this success, Bill Backer graduated to a position at McCann's – now the Coca-Cola agency – where he quickly found a niche writing what he called 'song-form commercials' for radio and TV. In 1963 he coined the line 'Things go better with Coke'. The upbeat jingle was originally sung by The Limelighters, but as the sixties progressed, and Robert Woodruff finally allowed Coca-Cola advertising to feature African-Americans, variations on the theme were performed by Ray Charles, The Supremes, Aretha Franklin, Marvin Gaye, and others. The campaign was in tune with the times, appealed to the youth market, and kept Pepsi well in its place. Woodruff had always insisted, after all, that 'The purpose of Coca-Cola advertising is to be liked'.

But by 1968 the campaign was running out of steam, and the world changing very fast around it. That's when Backer resurrected the old line, 'It's the real thing', and crafted a sequence of new commercials, already described, that brought this to life in a contemporary, laid-back context. It was as an extension of this campaign, rather than any quest for radical change, that in 1971 McCann's signed up a British/Australian vocal group, The New Seekers, to record some new radio commercials in a London studio. To co-write the material, they also engaged the British hit-writing duo of Roger Cook and Roger Greenaway; these were to work alongside Backer, together with another McCann's creative staffer, Roquel 'Billy' Davis. Davis came from Detroit, and had been an early member of The Four Tops; he had written numerous hit records, including Jackie Wilson's 'Reet Petite' and 'Higher and Higher'.

Only five days before they were due to go into the studio, Davis, Cook and Greenaway were together in London, waiting for Backer to join them. So far, they hadn't actually written anything for the New Seekers to record. The timing was tight, but the four experienced songsmiths must have been confident they had long enough to come up with the goods. However, Backer failed to arrive as expected; his flight was diverted to Ireland because of heavy fog at Heathrow, and he was stuck at Shannon Airport for two days, along with a jumbo jet load of other people anxiously bound for London or Frankfurt.

Unable to leave the airport, Backer observed how tempers frayed and some passengers became angry and argumentative. Then he noticed something else:

> By mid-morning all the shopping that could be done had been done, and the passengers began collecting in small groups around the tables in the coffee shop. A large, shapely German woman in her early thirties who had been one of the more indignant passengers was now sitting with a small Jewish businessman. In a loud, Teutonic manner she had demanded special treatment in the motel lobby the night before. The businessman and several other passengers had been openly contemptuous of her behaviour...

> And now, today, they were together, keeping each other company. Their common language seemed to be English with heavy accents, and the common icebreaker was a bottle of Coca-Cola (pp.5-6).

At this moment Backer had a new insight into Coca-Cola – it was not just a refreshing drink, but an image of 'commonality between diverse peoples'. On the plane he started doodling ideas for a song, and by the time he finally met up with his colleagues late the following day, he had a single line that he liked...

Their first reaction to it was lukewarm. Davis, who knew more than the others about poverty and the barriers between peoples, said that if he could buy the world anything, it wouldn't be a Coke, it would be a home. This eventually became the opening line, though no-one can remember who decided what to furnish it with. Cook pictured the orchard and the beehives; Backer brought in 'harmony' because he liked the word and it rhymed with 'company'. So, line by line, working steadily together into the night, they built the finished lyrics out of Backer's initial idea.

As the words came together, Greenaway and Davis found they already had a tune they had just written – to completely different words – and they fitted the two things together. So by the time they met the New Seekers in the studio a couple of days later, the song was complete. But when Backer heard them sing it, he wasn't happy. The tone wasn't right, and he had to work to get the feeling of innocence and simplicity that was needed: he didn't want it to sound 'like a jingle'. For their part, the singers pushed back on words that didn't 'sing right'. Despite the difficulties, a recording emerged they were all happy with.

It was launched across the USA as a radio commercial. And nothing much happened. It didn't attract much attention, and only a few listeners seemed at all enthusiastic. The song could easily have vanished without trace, but both Backer and his agency account director, Sid McAllister, believed it was somehow worth more than that. Over lunch they agreed that the powerful and new sentiment had simply got lost as a radio ad; as Sid said, 'They didn't get it' (or in Backer's words, 'our singing voices had no faces attached to them'). Against the odds, they persuaded the client that it should be re-imagined as a TV commercial.

But what would that actually mean? At that stage there was no hillside, no choir, no freckle-faced lead singer. A number of different visualisations were considered and rejected: block parties, biking holidays, neighbours getting acquainted, or the predictable idea of vignettes including all of the above. Then a young art director called Harvey Gabor walked into Backer's office and said,

> 'If there was such a thing as a United Chorus of the World, what would it look like?'

It didn't take long for Backer to feel this was the missing idea he'd been searching for. But this was not like anything Coke – or anyone else – had ever done before. And it turned out to be only the beginning of a tortuous process, one in which Backer was increasingly dependent on other allies to make things happen – art director Al Scully and agency producer Phil Messina being two. Meanwhile, at every stage, approval would be needed from the client to go ahead.

From the outset, Gabor had envisioned the scene in a real, beautiful landscape, not a limbo shot: this meant an expensive commercial, needing a large cast and helicopter shots. A multinational cast and a singer who could lip-synch to the New Seekers were duly recruited, and the shoot scheduled to take place on the White Cliffs of Dover. It poured with rain. Having used up his only day's weather insurance, the producer asked permission to move the entire shoot to sunny Italy. The sun shone, but the shoot was a total disaster. There were camera malfunctions that made most of the film unusable, and the hundreds of children who had been brought from orphanages to fill the final scene rioted after being cooped up in locked buses for hours.

But Sid McAllister was still prepared to support the project, and sanctioned a complete new shoot. There would be a new, Italian director and a local production company. Bill, Billy, Harvey, and Phil all knew this was their last chance to make it work. There was one outstanding problem: the actress who had been chosen to sing the opening lines in close-up had gone on honeymoon and was no longer available. All knew it was crucial to the film's success to get this casting right, yet the right look of naive idealism seemed impossible to find. Then Phil Messina spotted a nanny pushing a baby carriage across the Piazza Navona in Rome and knew she was the one. 19-year-old Linda Neary had never acted before, and it was with extreme difficulty that the team persuaded her to become the star in their commercial…

It would make a great movie, wouldn't it? Tom Hanks is sadly too old now for Bill Backer (who was in his mid 40s in 1971), but he'd make a fine Sid McAllister, and David Oyelowo could play a convincing Billy Davis, with Robert de Niro in a cameo role as Robert Woodruff. We can dream.

But although it's a good story, did 'Hilltop' actually sell any Coca-Cola? The answer to that question is – well, complicated.

It would be easy to conclude that the effect of 'Hilltop', and the many other less remembered commercials that preceded and followed it was, actually, not much. The fifteen years that followed teaching the world to sing were years in which Coke struggled to maintain share, and in which Pepsi-Cola grew its business with a succession of lively campaigns. Sergio Zyman, who worked at different times during this period for Coke's agency McCann, for Coca-Cola, and for Pepsi, later wrote a book about advertising in which he made his own judgments clear:

> In 1979 I joined the Coca-Cola Company in Atlanta, right at the time when Coke was heavy into entertaining and making emotional love to consumers.

That's when I found out exactly what happened after those ads I'd worked on at McCann… Nothing happened. All those beautiful, heart-grabbing, award-winning ads weren't having much of an effect…

And nearly 25 years later I'm still preaching the same message: Traditional advertising that only entertains doesn't work. (pp.12-13)

So, on the one hand, we have an experienced marketing director's conviction that 'Hilltop' was famous, but didn't sell any soda – another voice in that long tradition dating back to Claude Hopkins's 'people do not patronise a clown', and Earnest Elmo Calkins's condemnation of Sunny Jim. On the other hand, we have Douglas Holt, a respected academic, who sees 'Hilltop' as a redemptive moment that turned Coke's fortunes around. Who's right?

My guess is the truth lies somewhere in between. I've already qualified Holt's judgement of 'Hilltop', in that I see it as the most successful among a long series of successful commercials rather than a unique event. And I think its contribution needs to be evaluated in that context too – as part of a steady advertising pressure that maintained Coke's share and margin in the face of intense competition, even if this never showed up as an upward sales graph. Zyman simply doesn't recognise this, because like many marketers, he's only looking for short term growth as evidence of advertising effect.

But we also need to consider what might have happened if Coke had *not* advertised during this period, or even if their advertising had been less famous and likeable than it was.

Pepsi-Cola had been a very aggressive and effective competitor since their advertising guru Alan Pottasch began the 'Pepsi Generation' campaign in 1963. Before this, Coca-Cola had simply dominated the market, their heavy advertising followed by continuous growth as the US population and economy grew, and as Coke expanded into new territories around the world. Now they were in a new phase, in which the home market looked increasingly mature, and in which a strong competitor was giving them a real battle for brand share. It didn't help during this period that the management was beset with other problems that took their focus away from marketing, and that the antiquated relationship with 50,000 bottlers made decision making cumbersome and discouraged innovation.

So it may well have been the fact that Coca-Cola continued throughout this time to spend heavily, behind emotional, entertaining commercials, that ultimately prevented Pepsi-Cola from doing more damage than they did – because at the end of the day, Coke hardly lost any share to Pepsi, whose growth came more at the expense of other brands such as Royal Crown. I think it likely that 'Hilltop' and other films like it were just what Coke needed to hold their rival at bay. It's also likely – though again, we can't be sure without more data – that Coke's advertising helped to maintain their market share without excessive discounting. If that's so, it would have made a bigger difference to their bottom line than a minor increase in volume sales would have done.

If this hypothesis is true, it would certainly not be unusual. As I argued many years ago (1997b), the principal effect of advertising for mature brands in mature categories is to defend brand share and price against the competition. Byron Sharp agrees:

> The aim of most advertising is to maintain market share…Much advertising is aimed at preventing competitors' advertising from stealing future sales (p.137).

So the real question is not whether advertising *increased* share of volume, but how much revenue and profit would have been lost *without* advertising. Let's imagine a counterfactual history in which Coke basically stopped advertising altogether during the seventies, distracted from marketing and seeking to boost short term profits, a scenario in which 'Hilltop' would never have even happened. I find it all too easy to imagine that by the end of the decade the brand would have passed a point of no return, a permanent also-ran to Pepsi. In the short term, it's always easy to turn off the advertising tap and boost profits – as Ferdinand Schumacher did in the early years of Quaker Oats. But if Schumacher's strategy had persisted, Quaker Oats would today be no more remembered than any of the forgotten packaged oats brands that others launched but did not support.

The defensive role of advertising is not always recognised sufficiently by marketers who are, for both good and not so good reasons, usually much more interested in growth. Yet it's crucial to the long term survival of brands, and it is this long term resilience in terms of both price and market share that explains why brands have such a high value. A classic case from the UK that demonstrates this is the tea brand, P.G. Tips.

*

I've frequently begun university lectures on brands by posing the students a simple question. I tell them that in 1983, P.G.Tips had 23% of the UK tea market. I then ask them to guess what that figure might have been in 1984 – and sixteen years later, in 2001 – and sixteen years earlier, in 1969. (Try this yourself now if you want.)

Almost invariably, the guesses are highly volatile. Some imagine a trajectory from 50% or more in 1969 to a single digit share in 2001, others the opposite, while many assume the figures will randomly leap about, even between adjacent years. The students are usually astonished when I reveal that all four figures are either 23% or 24%. I admit I cheated a little, but not much – when I show a share graph spanning a forty year period, the line rises at one point to close on 30%, and elsewhere drops off to around 20%. (Significantly, the high point coincides with a few years of especially entertaining advertising, and the low point a period when advertising for the brand was cut back altogether.) But apart from these two episodes, every year is within two or three percentage points of 23%.

The students' responses show it's clearly not intuitive that brand share should remain so extremely stable over a long period of time – yet that is precisely one of the things that makes brands of such interest to business and to investors. I then point out to the students that during the period of this graph, quite apart from all the other changes that took place in the world between the sixties and the new century, important things happened in the UK tea market. There was a massive switch from leaf tea to tea bags, the retail trade shifted from mainly independents to dominance by a few supermarket chains, and those chains all launched own brands of tea that retailed for up to 50% less than P.G.Tips. Many other brands fought for share, advertising heavily, discounting, and innovating. The brand itself also changed ownership a couple of times. Yet, throughout all this, P.G.Tips maintained a steady share and a steady price premium, discounting less than its rivals. Though it is not a story of growth (tea consumption has steadily dropped in the UK since the fifties), for many years P.G.Tips was Unilever's biggest single profit earner in the UK.

Was this because the brand had access to a better product, or some other secret source of advantage? Not at all. Mixed with milk and sometimes sugar, it's virtually impossible to tell one black tea from another in blind tests. And we've already seen that P.G.Tips didn't compete on price. The only possible explanation for this brand's extraordinary and profitable resilience is its history of advertising, which throughout this period was highly popular, entertaining, and consistently built around a strong distinctive asset, the P.G. chimps. Companies do, of course, need growth, and the limitation of the P.G.Tips story is that nobody was able to find a way to extend the brand into new categories or territories that might have provided that growth. But let's not underestimate the importance of maintaining a profitable cash cow that is still delivering today after seventy years.

For those sceptics who still think this all sounds too whimsical and impressionistic, there is strong evidence that frequency of exposure to advertising is directly related to likelihood of purchase and so to business outcomes in the short term as well in the long term. From the seventies to the nineties, in a series of studies using single source panels (where media exposure and buying behaviour are recorded for the same individuals over time), Colin McDonald, Simon Broadbent, John Philip Jones and others consistently showed that in about half of all cases, exposure to an ad for Brand A shortly preceding a purchase occasion led to a significant increase in the probability of buying Brand A. This shows that the effect of brand advertising is not something that mysteriously only happens in the long term by some kind of mental accumulation (though this is almost certainly also true), but happens immediately, presumably by creating a short term rise in mental availability.

It therefore follows that maintaining a continuous weight of advertising relative to competition is of crucial importance, and this fact is supported by many observations that brands with a higher share of voice than share of market tend to grow, while those spending less than their share of market tend to decline

– this is known as the 'equilibrium share of voice' theory (ESOV), originally proposed by John Philip Jones and more recently confirmed by Les Binet and Peter Field. It seems that in advertising, as in other conflicts, God is usually on the side of the big battalions. And what appears superficially as a static situation may in reality be a fiercely contested battle for territory.

Some ads create a bigger effect than others, though most are broadly similar, with a smaller number of extreme outliers. It is also significant that, according to John Philip Jones's 1985 analysis, the most successful are 'intrinsically likeable... visual rather than verbal'. It seems that the most successful ads maintain both mental availability and liking when they are exposed sufficiently often. It is likely that this is just what happened both with P.G.Tips and with Coca-Cola, using ads which it is much more helpful to think of as a performance rather than a sales pitch.

Claude Hopkins insisted that the only role of advertising was to sell – 'It is not to help your other salesmen. It is not to keep your name before the public'. Yet these other things are precisely what the performance aspect of a brand does, and they make the actual selling much more efficient. A great performance doesn't automatically maximise revenue or profits, but it creates the potential for doing so. The pedlars, mountebanks and travelling medicine shows of yesteryear had to have products to sell, and techniques for closing the sales; but they knew that their selling was only made possible by the show, which gathered the audience, put them in the mood to buy, and eventually kept them loyal. Bill Backer knew this, and so – perhaps more importantly – did the autocratic Robert Woodruff, who frequently insisted to his staff that 'the purpose of Coca-Cola advertising is to be liked'.

The creation of a compelling performance requires a very different mindset from that required to run all the other aspects of a profitable business, though successful brands, of course, need both. One thing we might notice about the creation of 'Hilltop', as recalled by Bill Backer, is that at no point was there any talk of selling, of propositions or benefits, or even of strategy (cultural or otherwise). There is no mention in his account of a Creative Brief, a type of document which as far as I know hardly existed in US agencies at that time. The process the team engage in is serious work, serious enough to hire famous performers and top writers and fly people across the Atlantic and put them up in the Savoy Hotel, but the work is conceived above all as the creation of a piece of entertainment, a performance, not as a sales pitch. The debates that take place are about the integrity and the appeal of the performance, about its aesthetics. The casting of the lead singer is crucial, not because she has to represent the target audience or the 'brand essence', but because she needs a certain quality that is dictated by the work itself; in the same way, the location (which creates so many practical problems) is as it is because of the art director's purely aesthetic vision.

It's easy to understand why, from the point of view of anyone focused on business problems, market shares, or short term results, all this appears at best incidental, and perhaps even a kind of irrelevant self-indulgence. Ad agencies *can* be irrelevant and self-indulgent, and too often are. Yet the skills of putting on a show, of creating something distinctive and compelling which may have only the most tangential relationship to product or other concerns of the business, are commonly of central importance to creating the fame which makes brands so potentially lucrative and valuable. This putting on of a show is not simply a matter of decorating a product message or benefit, though it frequently appears to take that form; it is more fundamentally about creating a relationship, an emotional bond, or a social buzz, which will enhance the brand's 'saleability' – its likelihood of being chosen by more people in more situations, of being able to command a higher price, and in general of becoming more resilient to all the events which competitors or the environment can throw at it.

*

Conventional wisdom tries hard to simplify brands and advertising, and the processes for creating them. It reduces brands to an 'idea' or 'DNA', and adverts to 'propositions' or 'messages'. It also behaves as if brands and advertising have little or nothing in common with the broader environment of popular culture, media content, entertainment and celebrities in which they exist.

I hope it is clear by now that I seriously challenge this conventional wisdom. Brands principally grow as they become popular, and their popularity is qualitatively similar to that of celebrities, films, or hit records. Advertising is principally valuable because it is a controllable way of helping to create popularity. Popularity, fame, interest, and attractiveness are all qualities which both blur into and support each other. It is a crucial task for marketers and ad agencies to create and nurture them. But they are not created and nurtured by abstract ideas or essences; they are created and nurtured by actual performances, and by tangible distinctive assets.

I believe this is very consistent with the Ehrenberg-Bass theories of how brands grow and how advertising works. But we need to be careful what language we use. Byron Sharp has described advertising as 'mere publicity', and I myself referred in *The Anatomy of Humbug* to 'simple fame'. Such turns of phrase seem to imply that the creation of fame or popularity is a simple or trivial thing, but of course it's not. Popularity or fame are complex, emergent processes, that depend on far more than simply having a good idea, a catchy tune, a nice face or a better product – even though all these may help. As I hope my various examples have shown, brands grow, not with the inevitability of 'DNA' shaping a flower, but as the outcome of a complex sequence of gestures and responses, requiring sustained energy and adaptability over time. Compelling performances, which include advertisements, do not spring seamlessly from an abstract idea, but are created through complex processes of learning and adaptation, which require craft skills, aesthetic judgments, and a high tolerance of anxiety. Or to put all that more simply, it's showbusiness.

Coca-Cola, like the Beckhams, became famous through a fourfold combination of conditions:

- **Mass exposure:** From the outset, it set out to reach as large an audience as possible – its physical distribution being only one important part of this.

- **Attractive performance:** The product was attractive enough (perhaps especially in the early days when it had certain stimulating qualities), but never intrinsically that special – the fact that both Pepsi and New Coke were clearly preferred in blind tests should remind us that Coke's dominance was never really about the physical product. However, the brand has worked continually to create another kind of product that creates attraction, through its publicity – an ever evolving kaleidoscope of images, merchandise, songs, stories, and films, reflecting happy and inspiring fantasies and memories, whose purpose, as Robert Woodruff continually reminded his staff, 'was to be liked'.

- **Distinctive devices:** It has consciously created and nurtured a wide range of distinctive assets, from the script logo and classic bottle to Father Christmas and the polar bears.

- **Social diffusion:** Perhaps most of all, it has formed an important part of the social discourse, first in the USA and then in the whole world; people have made meanings out of Coke which have gone beyond any intended by the company itself, it has become a unique part of social behaviour, of shared meanings and memories, endlessly talked about, argued about, complained about, making news.

In Part Three, I shall have more to say about each of these four facets of fame.

Part Three

Four Facets of Fame

The great secret of success in anything is to get a hearing. Half the object is gained when the audience is assembled.

PHINEAS T.BARNUM, IN *GREAT HUMBUGS OF THE WORLD*

The stimulating thing about TV is your audience. Whatever you do on that bit of paper, 10 million people are going to see…that's wonderful.

10 million looking at your work… let's make it good.

JOHN WEBSTER

I was on one of my fruitarian diets. I had just come back from the apple farm. It sounded fun, spirited, and not intimidating. Apple took the edge off the word computer. Plus, it would get us ahead of Atari in the phone book.

STEVE JOBS, AS QUOTED IN WALTER ISAACSON'S BIOGRAPHY

Fama … mobilitate viget viresque adquirit eundo…

Fame thrives on her speed, and gains strength by going forward.

VIRGIL, *AENEID IV*

Chapter Nine

Broadcast to Go Big

In May 1954 Bill Haley and His Comets released a record called 'Thirteen Women', a distinctly unwoke masculine fantasy about being the only male left on earth after the 'H-Bomb' and so, apparently, an object of devotion for the remaining thirteen women.

The record sold a total of 75,000 copies – making it a very modest success compared to the band's earlier hit, 'Crazy Man Crazy', which had sold ten times that number. Despite the best efforts of the record company to promote it, the song more or less sank without trace, along with its flipside, a little number called 'Rock Around The Clock'. This was the song Haley had really wanted to record, but he'd had an uphill struggle to persuade his producer even to include it as a B-side. On the day of the studio session, a series of disasters and delays meant that it was very nearly never recorded at all. But despite making it on to 75,000 shellac discs, the song seemed destined for obscurity.

A few months later a Hollywood director, Richard Brooks, was working on his new film about the hot topic of 'juvenile delinquency', *The Blackboard Jungle*. One evening he visited the star of the film, his friend Glenn Ford, for drinks at his Beverley Hills home. Dick Brooks told Ford he wanted to open the movie with some of that new 'rock and roll' music, and asked him if he had any ideas for a suitably lively, edgy song. No, said Ford, but he thought his eleven year old son Peter might. The boy offered Brooks a few of his favourites, and the director chose 'Rock Around the Clock'. It would explode over the film's main title sequence, in a way that still packs a punch today.

When *Blackboard Jungle* was released the following year, it was a sensation. It wasn't the biggest grossing film of 1955, (it was number thirteen), but it was the most notorious. The newly identified 'teenagers' danced in the aisles at cinemas, blasted 'Rock Around The Clock' from their dorm windows, and generally scared the hell out of their parents, who had a full blown moral panic. Many cities banned the movie, which was seldom out of the news. And Bill Haley's record, now re-released as the A-side, went to the top of the Billboard charts, the first 'rock'n'roll' song to do so. It had an incalculable effect on the future of popular music and popular culture, and would eventually become the second biggest selling record of all time, after 'White Christmas'. It must be a signal of its pervasive global fame that one of my own earliest memories is of singing my own version of 'Rock Around The Clock' in our living room in Bideford, Devon, when I was three years old – even though my family had no record player, and the BBC Light Programme was the only popular music available on the wireless.

*

I found the back story of 'Rock Around The Clock' in American journalist Derek Thompson's 2017 book, *Hit Makers: How Things Become Popular*, where he tells it with a great deal more fascinating detail; he even went to the trouble of tracking down and interviewing Peter Ford sixty years after his fateful meeting with Dick Brooks. Following in the footsteps of Malcolm Gladwell's bestseller, *The Tipping Point*, from seventeen years earlier, Thompson weaves together a variety of real life case histories from the fields of entertainment and popular culture with scientific studies and experiments, to suggest answers to a question I've been hovering around: what is it that makes certain things massively famous and popular, while so many other, apparently similar things, never really take off?

One of Thompson's core themes is that there is nothing *inevitable* about anything becoming famous. It's easy to suppose that 'Rock Around The Clock' was always destined to be a worldwide hit because it was intrinsically a great record – yet before its use in *The Blackboard Jungle* it was a very moderate success. As we've already observed, fame does not automatically reward a great performance.

Should we, then, jump to the opposite conclusion, that fame is entirely a matter of chance and contingency? Up to a point: Thompson quotes an academic description of the entertainment business as 'a complex, adaptive, semi-chaotic industry with Bose-Einstein distribution dynamics and Pareto power law characteristics with dual sided uncertainty', which is a scientific-sounding way of admitting that there is no reliable way of predicting what becomes a hit, and that most things never will. And as in any kind of history, large consequences can turn on apparently trivial and random events: Dick Brooks's meeting with Peter Ford, or Bill Backer's fog-bound stopover at Shannon Airport.

It's also true that our perception of what constitutes 'a great performance' is massively influenced by fame itself. Because fame is a 'complex, adaptive, semi-chaotic' system it grows and evolves through time, and one of the important feedback loops within it is the fact that we rate things more highly as they increase in fame and familiarity. Because we prefer what is familiar, because we choose what comes more easily to mind, and because we are more attracted to what we see valued by others, things tend to become more attractive to us as they become better known and more popular. In the words of Jeremy Bullmore that I quoted earlier,

> ...for most human beings, fame not only holds a powerful fascination but bestows an incalculable value on anything that enjoys it. We value the famous far more highly than the little known.

Thompson provides the evidence and case studies to back this up, and while he mainly deals with artefacts of popular culture, he begins his book in the sphere of fine art. We probably suppose that the world's most popular and critically acclaimed paintings must have achieved their status inevitably, as a result of their intrinsic superiority. But it's not so. Researchers have shown that the canon of the most highly valued and popular Impressionist paintings can be *entirely* explained on the basis of which works happened to be in the influential collection of the lesser known impressionist painter, Gustave Caillebotte – even though Caillebotte collected only those paintings by his friends that nobody else much wanted. Fame creates liking and attractiveness, which in turn reinforces fame. As Thompson also shows, even the Mona Lisa was a relatively little known painting until it got into the news by being stolen, after which it was repeatedly lampooned by other artists.

Both 'Rock Around The Clock' and 'I'd Like to Teach the World to Sing' are now regarded as great, classic songs, but neither made much impact when originally released. It was only in the context of a much-talked-about film that each succeeded in achieving fame on a massive scale. Today, of course, we find it hard to imagine why either song flopped at first. But that's looking at it the wrong way round. The truth is that the high value we place on these songs today is largely a result of the familiarity and fame they subsequently achieved.

We can apply exactly the same principle to brands. The high value that people place on Coca-Cola or McDonald's or Apple or Nike or Google is in large part due to their very popularity. Our System 1 brains are especially comfortable with them because they feel so familiar to us, because they are readily 'available' to our minds, and because we are reassured by the social proof that their ubiquity and popularity implies. These biases (we could call them that) are surprisingly difficult to shift, which is why brands have such longevity and are worth such a great deal of money.

Our bias towards a famous brand *can* of course shift over time if the brand fails to maintain its fame through the mechanisms of publicity and promotion, but, on the whole, popular brands are remarkably resilient in the short or even medium term, capable of surviving lack of innovation, mediocre products or service, ethical concerns and consumer boycotts. Coke in the seventies was late to launch a diet-Cola, it had a product which was objectively inferior to its main rival, it had a cumbersome management structure and a risk-averse corporate culture. Yet it didn't really lose share of market.

So we come back to the idea that fame matters for brands: arguably, the most important thing that matters. Let's entertain that thought for a while and see where it might lead us. What lessons could brands learn (or perhaps remind themselves of) from studies of fame in the worlds of entertainment, fashion, and celebrity, such as *Hit Makers* or *The Tipping Point?* Because, despite the inescapable element of chance, if we understand which factors are generally necessary conditions for fame, we may least increase the odds in our favour.

Both Thompson's and Gladwell's inquiries separate the factors which enable fame into two groups. The first group includes all the intrinsic qualities of the performance itself which make it attractive and distinctive; the second group, the ways in which the performance becomes exposed to and is diffused among large populations. Both of these matter: both are usually necessary conditions for success. There are intrinsic qualities in a performance that significantly increase the chances of it becoming famous; but it will not become famous automatically as a result of these intrinsic qualities (except as a highly rare event).

In making this distinction, both authors draw explicit parallels with epidemiology. The spread of a disease can also be analysed as a function of two different kinds of factors. The first group of factors are to do with the intrinsic nature of the infecting organism – the way it is transmitted, how easily it is transmitted, how long it remains infectious in the carrier, etc. The second group of factors are contextual – these include environmental factors (e.g. the prevalence of anopheles mosquitoes for malaria, an infected source of water for cholera), and many social patterns of human behaviour which may either enable or inhibit the transmission of the disease, such as hygiene, travel, sexual activity, and so on.

Gladwell sums up this analogy at the outset of his book:

> ...the idea is very simple. It is that the best way to understand the emergence of fashion trends, the ebb and flow of crime waves...the transformation of unknown books into bestsellers, or the rise of teenage smoking, or the phenomena of word of mouth, or any number of the other mysterious changes that mark everyday life is to think of them as epidemics. *Ideas and products and messages and behaviours spread just like viruses do.* (p. 7, *emphasis added*)

The Tipping Point was itself a huge best seller, and very influential in marketing and advertising circles. I, like a thousand others, was given my own signed copy when I took part in the American Account Planning Group's conference in Miami in 2000, at which the author was the keynote speaker, and I remember first reading it excitedly on the plane home. (As a technique of diffusion among an influential sub-group, it worked: Gladwell was certainly practising what he preached.) It may not be coincidence, then, that as the internet became more all pervasive in the following years, and as social media platforms took off, so did the viral metaphor as a simple way to explain how things spread.

Gladwell was at pains to point out that in practice, the 'viral' diffusion of content or ideas nearly always depends on certain 'super-spreaders' or influencers who make connections with large numbers of people: he called this 'The Law of the Few', and he identified and named different types of influencer as Mavens, Connectors, and Salesmen. Yet the emphasis that I suspect most advertising readers took from his book (and then passed on more widely in an even more simplified form) was that 'virality' was an automatic process that largely took care of itself, once you had crafted a sufficiently interesting thing to be passed on.

For their own reasons, both agencies and marketers very much liked the idea that 'going viral' was the new thing. For marketers, it meant they could dispense with those inconveniently large media budgets; for agencies, they could get 'edgy' work out there which would never in a million years get through the copy clearance procedures of broadcast media (or in some cases, even through their clients: with no media to pay for, they might even fund it themselves in order to showcase their agency and win awards). Sometimes, up to a point, it seemed to work, especially as long as the whole area had the excitement of novelty about it.

But there was a huge amount of self-delusion about it all. Many of the case histories which agencies excitedly shared seemed to have no idea of the scale of the numbers they were talking about, boasting about views numbered in the hundreds or even just tens of thousands, while forgetting that this amount of reach was equivalent to a 3 a.m. spot on an infomercial channel or a single newspaper insertion in one provincial town. Some did better, but even a much-awarded case like the Volkswagen sponsored 'piano staircase' of 2009, which was claimed to have reached 17 million people worldwide, was only reaching the equivalent of a couple of peak TV spots in two or three countries. More importantly, the implicit 'viral' myth ignored the fact that most of those who did look up this video would have been made aware of it through the extensive press coverage which the story received: in other words, through broadcast events rather than 'virality'. Nothing wrong with any of that, as far as it goes – it was a stunt designed to get exposure at a low cost, and up to a point it succeeded – but it didn't really go very far.

If Gladwell stimulated a widespread belief in 'virality', the emphasis in Thompson's book is the other way about. While he is, in a sense, merely repeating another version of Gladwell's 'Law Of The Few', he cites the evidence that online 'virality' as it's commonly understood doesn't really happen to any meaningful extent. The case history from epidemiology that he chooses to recount at length is the story of the Broad Street Pump, in which John Snow plotted the exact location of cholera cases in London's Soho in the nineteenth century, and discovered that the disease was not spread from person to person, nor through 'miasma' in the air, but could be attributed to one particular source of water. Not all infectious diseases, of course, spread in the same way as cholera, but for Thompson this becomes a useful metaphor for what's generally true in the field of fame: he shows in convincing detail how both the Harry Potter books and the *Fifty Shades of Grey* series did not achieve massive scale just by sharing between one individual and another, but through a series of 'mass contamination events' which hugely multiplied the numbers exposed to them. And he cites academic studies into what really happens online:

> On the Internet, where it seems like everything is going viral, perhaps very little or even nothing is. [The researchers] concluded that popularity on the Internet is 'driven by the size of the largest broadcast'. Digital blockbusters are not about a million one-to-one moments as much as they are about a few one-to-one-million moments (p.190).

The illusion of 'virality' is easily maintained because these instances of 'broadcast diffusion' often go unnoticed. In 2012, for instance, I might have received from a friend a link to a video about Joseph Kony, the Ugandan rebel leader, which received over 100 million views on YouTube within a few days. I would not have been aware that the chances of my friend being aware of the video in the first place depended entirely on the fact that it had been previously shared by a few individuals with many millions of followers, like Kim Kardashian or Justin

Bieber: examples of what Thompson calls 'dark broadcasters'. It is, to be fair, the 'Law of The Few' again, though at the time Gladwell was writing there were no social media platforms to enable any individuals to reach such enormous networks. Celebrities and influencers with millions of online followers are a recent phenomenon, but in effect they are just a new kind of broadcaster.

So I propose that for practical purposes, one essential element in creating mental availability on a large scale is access to mass, broadcast events. This is by no means the *only* thing necessary – ads can appear on the Superbowl, records be played on the airways, shows air on peak time television and can all be as instantly forgotten as yesterday's newspaper headlines. Indeed most of them do. Yet it seems important to stress that 'mass contamination events' are almost always a *necessary* part of the process, if only to wean ourselves away from the belief that, if you get the 'content' right, fame will automatically follow because everyone who comes across it will pass it on in some kind of exponential chain reaction. For all practical purposes we ought to assume that this isn't really going to happen.

As Thompson neatly sums it up:

> Almost nothing really goes viral, but some ideas and products really are more infectious than others. They are shared and discussed at higher-than-average rates. *But to go big, they need that broadcast* – the Walmart book stand, the Kardashian tweet, the proverbial water pump – to push them into the mainstream, *where people will find them and share them* (p.197, *emphasis added*).

The missing link between infectious content and widespread social diffusion, then, has to be one or more 'mass contamination events'. These might just happen by chance, as *The Blackboard Jungle* propelled 'Rock Around the Clock' from an obscure B-side to a massive hit. But if we want them to happen to us – to our brand, band, or movie – there are ways we must try to engineer them.

The simplest, most controllable way, but also the most costly, is by paying money – buying advertising time and space, product placement, paying 'influencers', buying in-store display or paying for inclusion on playlists (some kinds of payment for exposure may be restricted by regulations or laws, though they may still happen clandestinely). Less expensive, but also less controllable, are ways of engineering access to mass audiences without directly paying for them: Barnum's tradition of creating stories which the newspapers could not resist covering, built on and refined by Edward Bernays and generations of the best PR consultants; negotiating to appear in contexts that already have a mass audience (like Chuck Berry on the *Beech Nut Show*, the Spice Girls at The Brits, Joe Sugg taking part in *Strictly*, getting your book chosen by Oprah, or Richard and Judy); the whole behind-the-scenes world of agents, the use of networks of contacts, of mutual trust and reciprocal favours (this too can have its shadow side). If you own access to a mass audience yourself you may of course make use of that at minimal cost: again, Barnum understood this well, and continually invested in his own fame in order to make use of it; today, Kylie Jenner can launch a range of cosmetics entirely through her own followers (which also automatically earns more coverage elsewhere), Google is in a strong position to launch Gmail, or Apple a games platform.

These three approaches have in recent years been labelled as paid for, earned and owned media. Perhaps the most reliable approach is to make use of all three, as the safest route to fame has always been to do as much as possible. One of the core strategic principles of the British Armed Forces is called The Principle of Redundancy. The idea is that if you are fighting a war there is no point in trying to optimise efficiency – the only thing that matters is winning. The more tanks, the more aircraft, the more drones, the more ammunition, the more field hospitals you have, the better your chances. Rather than ask 'how cheaply can we do this?', the question is 'how much can we possibly get and how much can we possibly deploy?'. This idea runs completely counter to modern business's obsession with efficiency, yet it tends to characterise the major land-grabs of fame. A hundred years ago, Coca-Cola won territory in the soft drinks market it has held ever since by endlessly multiplying its mental and physical availability; in the present century, Amazon has won what currently looks like an unassailable position in online retailing by investing more than it makes every year into growing the business. Barnum did not launch Jenny Lind's tour by booking three concerts to 'see how it went' – he almost bankrupted himself in committing to 150, and as a result they all sold out. Excess and apparent wastage are not just important because they accelerate the gain of a dominant position – they also add in themselves to the creation of fame, notoriety, and respect.

Like the peacock's tail, a spectacle of conspicuous waste commands admiration (Ambler and Hollier). If there is a choice to be made between efficiency and thinking big, you cannot afford to be efficient if you want to be famous.

So I believe mass communication events should be considered necessary in any strategy for creating fame. But they are not sufficient. We also need to consider what factors make content 'infectious'. What are the qualities that make something enjoyable or interesting enough for people to spend time with it, remember it, value it, and share it with others? And what kind of processes and cultures are more likely to produce such content?

Chapter Ten
Make the Monster Massive

It would have been sometime in late 1975 that I remember riding on the top deck of a London bus, probably having a smoke on my way to the agency, as I became aware of a group of children behind me on their way to school. They were taking it in turns to raise their shoulders, roll their eyes, and intone in the deepest voice they could manage 'Tell'em about the Honey, Mummy!' at which point all would collapse in fits of laughter. And I felt a quiet glow of satisfaction. Perhaps the business I had somehow ended up in was not completely irrelevant to people's lives.

My agency, Boase Massimi Pollitt (BMP), had just launched a new TV campaign for a breakfast cereal called Sugar Puffs, owned by Quaker Oats. Sugar was already becoming a bit of a dietary turn-off, so we had chosen to associate the product with honey instead, which was seen as better for your kids. Our Creative Director, John Webster, had created a character called Honey Monster – larger than a human, covered in yellow fur, wearing a baseball cap and with all the characteristics of a five year old apart from his deep bass voice, he lived with a man whom he took to be his Mummy. Yes, it was all very odd. But it was immediately hugely popular, as my experience on the bus indicated. It also sold a lot of Sugar Puffs, and Honey Monster is still the brand's well-known mascot today.

You may think it is a pointless exercise to attempt any analysis of just what it was about those ads that made Honey Monster such a popular success – another attempt at 'murdering to dissect'. I have some sympathy. But I also think it is possible to look at some of the characteristics of this campaign, qualities it has in common with many other popular hits (as suggested by Derek Thompson and others). It's also possible – and perhaps even more useful – to pay attention to the processes and conditions which enabled this campaign to be made. We can be confident we will never succeed in reducing its particular charm and appeal to any set of formulas, but we can do better than simply dismissing it with words like 'intuition', 'art', or 'magic' – the kind of words, which, as Don Schön once said, exist to close down discussion rather than invite it. In that spirit, here are some observations – by no means exhaustive – about what it is that made the Honey Monster campaign such an immediate popular success.

*

The commercial that introduces Honey Monster is set in a kitchen that looks like the set for a children's TV show – very simple, primary colours, a table that's a little too large to be realistic. Behind the table, looking slightly embarrassed, stands the actor Henry McGee, best known at that time as a 'straight man' to comedians like Benny Hill and Charlie Drake. At his side, on the left of the screen, is Honey Monster, a hulking figure who is shyly avoiding eye contact and tapping his foot on the floor like a small child reluctant to perform in public.

McGee: I'd like to introduce you to – Honey Monster.

HM (*in a deep bass voice, putting his arm around McGee*): Mummy!

McGee: I'm *not* his mummy. Now, to help a Honey Monster through the morning, I give him breakfast including Sugar Puffs and milk.

HM (*who has been giggling throughout this speech*): Tell 'em about the honey, Mummy!

McGee: Pieces of natural wheat, puffed up, and tasting of honey.

HM (*more and more excited*): Honey! They taste of honey! I love my honey! I love my mummy! (*In his excitement he hits the table which immediately collapses*).

Cut to a shot of McGee (*now reclining in the Honey Monster's arms*): So, if anyone asks why Sugar Puffs taste so good, remember:

HM (*in final close up*): Tell 'em about the honey, Mummy.

There are a number of ideas from Derek Thompson's *Hit Makers* that we could apply to this commercial.

1   Balance between familiarity and novelty.

One of Thompson's main themes is that people get pleasure from two contradictory experiences. One is familiarity, because it makes us feel safe; the other is novelty, or challenge, because it stimulates our energy. A great deal of what becomes most popular gets just the right balance between the two. Too much challenge on its own is alienating and stressful – too much familiarity is simply boring. Hits combine both. Many others have independently come to this kind of conclusion: Thompson cites Professor Paul Heckert's 'Unified Model of Aesthetics', and, at greater length, the great designer Raymond Loewy's touchstone acronym, MAYA ('Most Advanced Yet Acceptable').

The Honey Monster launch commercial fits this pattern. There's a lot about it that's weird and challenging, certainly the first time you ever see it: where did this monster come from? why is he dressed like a child? what's his relation with this man? why does he call him 'Mummy'? (I personally remember seeing this film for the first time before it went on air and thought it would completely alienate the audience – not for the last time, my judgment was spectacularly wrong.) But there's also much that's very familiar. Henry McGee was a familiar face, and most of what he's doing lies firmly within the framework of the most traditional kind of TV commercial, a presenter, in a kitchen, talking to camera about the product's qualities. Honey Monster himself combines familiar elements in slightly unexpected ways: he's furry like a teddy bear, has huge appealing eyes like many lovable characters, he recognisably dresses and acts like a child though he has a deep bass voice (this combination of recognisable but contradictory things is also part of what makes him comical).

You may think this point is too general to be of much practical use. But if we contrast it with the characteristic language that ad agencies today tend to use about what they consider 'great work', which places a one dimensional emphasis on originality, 'disruption', shock and controversy, we can see how easily the notion of balance or 'MAYA' can be lost, and with it the ability to become popular.

In his excellent book, *Copy, Copy, Copy,* Mark Earls argues at length that most successful artistic or scientific achievements owe much more to copying others than our modern obsession with 'originality' would imply. In a detailed analysis of Elvis Presley's early work, he points out that just about all his records were covers of songs already recorded by others, and that even gestures that he would come to be closely associated with were copied from other performers. This is not to belittle his achievement or his talent. As Earls says, Elvis 'remains for most of us The Original, The King, The One and Only'. His 'originality', if we are to call it that, lay in his unique personal artistry, his ability to combine elements from different styles and different performers, and the mysterious alchemy that formed something new out of many things that already existed. But without that solid basis of the already familiar, it's hard to imagine that Elvis would ever have been a popular success.

2   The use of story

Related to this combination of familiarity and challenge is the way this commercial uses a story. It has been said that there are two narrative drives in any kind of fiction: what is going to happen, and what has happened? In just thirty seconds, this ad manages to include both. In the narrative that we see enacted, the presenter's attempt to talk directly to the audience about the product is repeatedly interrupted and eventually subverted by Honey Monster, a build-up of comic tension that reaches a climax with the table collapsing and is then resolved with the Monster holding Henry McGee protectively in its arms.

But there's another story which is never fully explained – how did these characters get into this situation, why does Honey Monster think the man is his Mummy? This poses the viewer a kind of riddle, one which will not be resolved for them, at least within the commercials themselves (though John Webster did himself always have an elaborate back story about how the Honey Monster was rescued from an island by Henry McGee and, never having known his real mother, always assumed that he must be her). But it's the sort of riddle that also creates a pleasurable anticipation that at some future point it might be resolved, a forward narrative drive that keeps people watching and thinking about it; and after a while, as the situation becomes more familiar, people no longer find it so strange, or create their own solution. Initial disfluency gives way to fluency, a pleasurable moment that another of Thompson's experts calls the 'aesthetic aha'.

Again, this may seem an over-elaborate analysis of something we experience as quite simple. But if we contrast it with many of today's TV commercials we will find that in these there is often no discernible narrative at all, merely a sequence of disconnected images, an experience of disfluency which alienates us rather than offering us an invitation to resolve it. In Thompson's own words, 'people actually prefer complexity – up to the point that they stop understanding something… they like complex mysteries with narrative puzzles that come to completion.'

3   Rhythm and assonance.

The principle of familiarity combined with the right amount of novelty also applies to many verbal or musical structures that become popular. Using melody, rhythm, assonance, and rhyme, songs, slogans and speeches that succeed characteristically combine patterns of repetition (pleasing familiarity) with just enough divergence from the predictable to keep us interested. Thompson finds these kind of patterns in ancient rhetorical techniques and in modern speechwriters, in the choruses of pop songs, and in political and advertising slogans.

John Webster was a master at creating bits of language that had just these qualities. A couple of years before Honey Monster, he had written a line for

Pepsi-Cola which was set to lively, rhythmic music and appeared at the end of each Pepsi commercial:

Lipsmackinthirstquenchinacetastinmotivatin

goodbuzzincooltalkinhighwalkinfastlivin

evergivincoolfizzinPepsi

This combines the pleasure of a regular and energetic pulse with a subtle and complex pattern of rhythm and assonance which is never predictable, balancing the regularity with constant interest. It also poses a challenge – to repeat it or memorise it – an invitation which a generation of teenagers spontaneously took up and so created a wave of social diffusion which further enhanced the slogan's popularity.

There is something similar in the Sugar Puffs commercial too. 'Tell 'em about the honey, Mummy', has a clearly defined and memorable rhythm, with a regular pulse which is offset by not being exactly the same in each bar:

/Tell *'em a*/bout *the* /honey, /Mummy/

and 'honey' and 'Mummy' have plenty of assonance (through the vowel sounds), while they don't actually rhyme.

These kind of verbal/musical patterns achieve two (related) outcomes: they give us a kind of pleasure, and they are easy to memorise. Such slogans therefore enable the creation of strong, distinctive, mental associative networks. They also invite participation and repetition, adding to their social diffusion. Hence, my experience on the bus.

So the Honey Monster commercial clearly shares key factors for success with other popular successes of the sort that Thompson examines in *Hit Makers*. I don't imagine that John Webster constructed any of this in a calculated way. Like other successful entertainers, he intuitively grasped what sort of thing was likely to be popular. But it would also be misleading to suppose that the Honey

Monster campaign in its finished form simply emerged from John's immensely talented brain without any other input.

In a memorial volume privately printed by the agency after John Webster's untimely death (a very fit 71, he had a heart attack while running), we can find an account by BMP account planner Sarah Carter of how the campaign was created.

> In those days, BMP had a particular way of briefing creative teams, which they called 'narrative creative briefing'. There was no fixed creative brief form... Instead, after spending hours conducting numerous groups with the target audience of the brand in question, planners just wrote a paragraph or two on a bit of paper. This acted as an aide memoire to the important bit – which was the verbal briefing to creative teams.
>
> This narrative briefing was made for John. The planner would sit on the sofa in John's corner office and talk for half an hour or so. And John would listen intently – he was a fantastic listener – and he loved nothing more than hearing anecdotes and quotes from the groups...
>
> In the Sugar Puffs briefing, John's ears pricked up when Chris [Mitchell, the planner] mentioned that mums often referred to their kids as their 'little monsters'. He hadn't heard this before and it intrigued him.
>
> This formed the basis for John's idea for Sugar Puffs: monsters who were desperate to eat Sugar Puffs.

Before we go on, it may be helpful to explain the next step in our creative process at the time, as several aspects of it are very different from what is usual today. The 'groups' already referred to – we never called them 'focus groups' – were groups of around eight consumers recruited to fit specific criteria (e.g. mums, Sugar Puffs non-users, or children 7-8 years old). The groups were held in the recruiters' houses, hardly ever in viewing facilities, and lasted about ninety minutes. The planners nearly always moderated the groups themselves, in a fairly non-directive way. We would conduct several groups at an early exploratory stage, as here, to get an understanding of our audiences, the language they used, the ways they related to the product, the ads they liked, and so on.

We'd then take out an early version of the ads to find out how they responded to these. The ads were always presented as 'animatics'. In these, the visuals were represented as a series of drawings, which were then shot under a rostrum camera and synchronised to a real-time soundtrack which could include dialogue, voice over, sound effects, and music. Naturally some nuances were lost by using drawings rather than a finished film, but the overall effect matched very closely the experience of watching a thirty second commercial in real time.

The whole process was logistically much more complex than it would be today. Domestic video recorders did not exist. As planners, we lugged around with us our own Philips VCRs (a system now long obsolete) together with a TV monitor to set up in the recruiters' living rooms. To make an animatic took several days and involved commissioning an artist (there was one guy called Harry we used whenever we could because he was brilliant at it), setting up a recording session, and then putting it all together. Despite the amount of effort involved, it was agency policy at that time that every TV commercial, without exception, should be subject to this kind of research – after some embarrassing early mistakes, Martin Boase and Stanley Pollitt had been convinced that nobody's 'creative judgment' could substitute for observing the responses of the real target audience.

So this was what happened with John's Sugar Puffs ads:

> …the first incarnation of the idea didn't work at all. In the first animatic, the monster was portrayed as child-sized. This came back from the research as all wrong on two fronts; children said it was wrong because monsters are meant to be huge and crash through walls and smash through windows. The mums didn't like it either because the monster was seen as a bad role model – reminding them of a badly behaved child…

> After listening to the findings from the planner, John had a simple but inspired idea.

> 'Let's make the monster massive.'

> This immediately changed the monster from destructive (bad) to clumsy (endearing).

Consumer feedback is not a panacea for popular success. There are many ways it can be done clumsily, or interpreted without insight or imagination (most usually, because it is fixated on the wrong model of advertising). But done well, as we demonstrated many times, it can contribute enormously to the chances of creating a hit. In *The Tipping Point*, Malcolm Gladwell devotes a long section to the creation of the educational puppet show, *Sesame Street*, and how it became (in his word) 'sticky'. He shows how through rigorous research with groups of children – not unlike what we were doing with our ads – the creators of the series came to revise just about all their basic assumptions about what children would find engaging and compelling. All the 'experts' had said that children wouldn't understand mixing puppets with live characters – yet it turned out that this was actually the only way to maintain their involvement through the show. A whole range of insights hinged on the fact that the children's experiences, what they found funny or alienating, what made sense or simply baffled them, were just completely different from what the writers had imagined they would be. This was exactly what we found, time and again, through our use of animatics in group discussions.

Central to this was one important fact: our guiding principle was to make work that would be popular, we genuinely wanted people to enjoy our ads. Certainly, although John Webster loved winning awards, I believe his real motivation was creating something that would be laughed about and endlessly repeated in the pub or the playground. I am not sure how many people or agencies in advertising today share that clarity of intention; I suspect some of them actively want to avoid being seen to be too 'popular'.

Given that intention, we had somehow, for the most part tacitly, evolved ways of working that very often succeeded: approaching a piece of advertising with much of the same mindset that you would approach a piece of entertainment, with a focus on narrative, character, humour, and the memorable use of language, and continually adjusting this as we observed the audience response.

I've concentrated in this chapter on the characteristics of a popular success that create pleasure for the audience. But equally important – and by no means entirely separate from the pleasure principle in any case – are those characteristics that make it distinctive and memorable. As these are especially important for brands and for advertising, we will deal with this topic in the next chapter.

Chapter Eleven

Give the Lion Wings

Venice today is a beautiful crumbling backwater, with an uncertain future. But for over a thousand years it was the centre of one of the world's most powerful trading empires, with shipyards that could build and fit out a warship in a single day. The image of the winged lion, which appears not just all over Venice but throughout the eastern Mediterranean, symbolises its dominance in a particular and unique way – it's not just a lion, with its connotations of strength and right to rule, but a lion with wings, a lion that could cross the sea at a moment's notice to wreak vengeance.

The Lion of Venice, like all the best symbols, is an image with many meanings, suggesting for example both peaceful rule and warlike anger, both beauty and strength – yet the power of the image itself immediately transcends any words that we attempt to reduce it to. Perhaps if the winged lion had never been, the history of Venice would have been exactly the same. But, as I tend to believe that visual symbols have a particular kind of power, I can't help feeling that, over the centuries, this image must have played an important role in creating the shared identity of the Venetians themselves, and in enabling them to project their power over others.

It might be amusing to imagine that a Venetian committee of PR and branding experts sat down together, sometime in the ninth century, and drew up a 'brand onion' for the City-State around words like 'strength', 'fierceness', or 'rapid response'. Of course, nothing like this ever happened. So what were the circumstances that led to the Venetians' adoption of this powerful symbol?

By the ninth century, as Venice was growing in power and influence, its rulers decided they needed a more prestigious patron saint than the rather obscure dragon-slayer, St Theodore. (His statue can still be seen on one of the columns in the Piazzetta, leading what looks very like a crocodile on a leash.) So in 858 C.E., two Venetian merchants stole the remains of St Mark the Evangelist from Alexandria, and installed them in the Doge's private chapel on the Rialto. Relics were a big sign of power in those days, and owning an actual evangelist made Venice almost up there with Rome.

The Venetians then made up a back story about why St Mark had always been their patron saint. During his lifetime, they insisted, he had travelled to the Venetian lagoon, where he had a dream in which an angel said to him 'Pax tibi Marce, evangelista meus. Hic requiescet corpus tuus'. (Peace be to you, Mark, my evangelist. Here may your body rest.)

But what has St Mark to do with the winged lion? Well, there is a strange passage in the first chapter of Ezekiel where the prophet has a vision of four winged beasts, with the faces of a man, a bull, a lion, and an eagle. The early fathers of the Christian Church were keen to explain as much as possible of the Old Testament as a prophecy of Christ, so in this tradition St Jerome, writing in the fifth century, decided the four beasts must represent the authors of the four Gospels, and identified St Mark with the lion.

The process of visualising St Mark's patronage as a winged lion was helped further when, at some unspecified date, Venetian travellers in what is now southern Turkey found a massive bronze figure of a winged lion or griffin dating from about 300 BC, and brought it home with them. This strange beast, which since 1285 has stood on the other column at the entrance to St Mark's Square, opposite St Theodore, may well have been the origin of the Venetian logo. The lion, now embellished with an open book containing the words 'Pax tibi Marce...', soon became the motif on the Venetian banner, and over time was copied all over the city and its empire. Its significance is underlined by the fact that, when Napoleon overthrew the Venetian republic, he gave orders for all the winged lions in the city to be destroyed. Fortunately, this order was not fully executed.

The story interests me because although the lion with wings has become a symbol with layers of apparently relevant meanings, its original selection came about for a series of entirely fortuitous reasons. In this respect it is not alone. As, in a final irony, the 'Lion of St Mark' today also happens to be one of the most prestigious creative awards in advertising, we may perhaps be allowed to imagine it as the ancestor of all those furry animals that have acted as brand symbols ever since: the PG Chimps and their successor 'Monkey', the Cresta Bear, the Hofmeister Bear, the Honey Monster, the Dulux sheepdog, the Andrex puppy, and most recently Alexandr Orlov and the other Meerkats.

In every one of these cases, the animal was chosen not because it somehow stood for abstract qualities that were to be associated with the brand, but through random chains of association, or even mere chance, that are no more straightforward than those leading to the Lion of Venice. The Dulux sheepdog, an image so universally associated with the paint brand in the UK that examples of the breed are often called 'Dulux Dogs', appeared quite by chance as a last minute prop in an otherwise unmemorable TV commercial, sometime around 1960. Probably because it was the only thing viewers found interesting, the dog re-appeared in other ads and eventually became synonymous with the brand. In the process it took on, like the winged lion, a rich range of implicit meanings – warmth, homeliness, family, trustworthiness, comfort – all very useful values to shift associations of paint away from chemical smells and towards a vision of the ideal family home. Yet none of these meanings had been intended; they simply emerged over time.

The Andrex puppy had an even more fortuitous origin. The original plan for the commercial, in 1972, was to have a young girl running to the bottom of the garden unspooling a toilet roll to demonstrate its extra length – a simple product benefit demonstration. At the last minute, the ITV copy clearance committee decided it wasn't acceptable, worrying that small children all over the country would copy this behaviour and ITV would get all the complaints. With the shoot booked and very little time, the inspired idea of substituting a puppy was approved, and the choice of a Labrador was pretty much dictated by what was available at short notice.

But this last-minute workaround proved hugely successful. The puppies (there were soon more than one) were cute and charming and the public couldn't get enough of them. Many people must have assumed they had been chosen to represent 'softness', an association that was soon made explicit, though this had never been part of the original intention. Nearly fifty years on, they continue to be associated with the brand.

In 1955 the copywriter briefed to write one of the first ever British TV commercials, for P.G. Tips tea, went for a walk around London Zoo in search of inspiration. In those days it was considered funny to dress the chimpanzees up in human clothes and make them act out a 'tea party', and watching this gave him the idea for an ad – chimps in an English country house having a posh afternoon tea, with a voice-over archly delivered by Peter Sellers. I doubt if he or anyone else imagined that this campaign would run for more than forty years – and today, when the idea of performing chimps is no longer acceptable to many, has been replaced by a Monkey sock puppet (who, incidentally, was originally created for another brand altogether, which had sadly gone bust).

John Webster was a master of creating brand characters, especially furry animals like Honey Monster. He created George the Bear for Hofmeister, a German lager brand with an existing bear logo which George referred to as 'a picture of my grandpa'. A few years earlier, John had invented the Cresta Bear, an animated polar bear with a deep-voiced American accent who went into noisy spasms when he drank the fizzy drink. When John Webster first presented it, the client is reported to have asked in bewilderment – 'Why a polar bear?', to which John replied: 'Why not?' (Presumably the same lack of logic led to Coca-Cola, years later, developing a highly successful commercial full of polar bears which have also become recognisable brand properties.)

Furry animals however are only one sub-set of a larger group, brand characters; which are themselves only one small part of the category which Jenni Romaniuk of the Ehrenberg-Bass Institute has identified as 'distinctive brand assets'.

Distinctive assets can be visual – characters, celebrities, logos, colours, fonts, and many other images; they can be verbal, such as slogans, catchphrases, accents; they can be audible, like sound effects, recognisable voiceovers, jingles, and music generally; they can exist in just about any modality, or any combination of modalities. Distinctive assets are powerful ways for a brand to maintain mental availability, when they are both famous and uniquely associated with the correct brand.

I think the concept of distinctive assets can be applied to any kind of fame. Celebrities each have a ready-made distinctive asset in their own face, though many add importantly to this with other aspects of personal styling – Bill Haley's kiss curl, Elvis's quiff, Freddy Mercury's moustache, even Donald Trump's lurid comb over. Geri Halliwell's Union Jack dress, Charlie Chaplin's bowler hat and cane, James Dean's overcoat all have aspects of distinctive assets, and so of course do personal catchphrases and individual accents: if I mention a red fez and the words 'Just Like That!' spoken in a northern accent, most British readers will know who I mean. But because examples are so universally easy to find, in this chapter I shall focus on distinctive assets used by brands, and especially in advertising.

Jenni Romaniuk's book on the subject is full of insights, evidence, and practical guidelines for the management of distinctive brand assets, and it's not my intention to summarise it all here (go and read it). But there are a couple of specific points I'd like to link to some of what I've said so far.

Romaniuk reminds us that the purpose of distinctive assets is, by definition, to be distinctive – not to be meaningful. Trying to build assets around some 'meaning' that you want your brand to have is more likely to fail, because your brand's meaning is probably very close to that of all your competitors. (You will recall Ehrenberg-Bass's core finding that brands are differentiated far less than many marketers like to imagine.) To invent an example, if Starbucks had decided to build its logo around a coffee bean, it would have created a very weak and indistinctive asset. By choosing instead a siren, a mermaid with two tails, an image with no logical connection to coffee and only a very tangential link to the name Starbuck (originally a character in *Moby Dick*), they now have a sign that few people would ever mistake for any other brand.

This may be one way of explaining why so many of the great distinctive assets that brands have acquired over the years so often appear to have emerged through happenstance, or mere playfulness. A purely arbitrary visual symbol (or melody, or typeface) will generally be more distinctive than anything that has been over-thought. Great distinctive assets are not so much created as accepted and nurtured.

This is because a distinctive asset only has one real job to do – to evoke the brand name, not the category. In a slogan, the link to the brand name may be built in:

> Should've gone to Specsavers.

Or Dave Trott's great line from the eighties,

> Hullo Tosh! Got a Toshiba?

Or, an example given by Malcolm Gladwell:

> 'Cause my Winstons taste good/ Like a cigarette should.

(Gladwell believes one reason this caught on was the unusual, ungrammatical use of the word 'like'. Romaniuk's more rigorous analysis also suggests that unusual words in slogans add to their uniqueness and fame.)

But it doesn't have to be: most of us will find it just as easy to identify the brand in

> It's the Real Thing

> Because I'm Worth It

> You're not you when you're hungry

Visually too, an asset may be a representation of the brand name, like the Coca-Cola 'script' logo – which as we've seen, was spontaneously drafted in the very early years of the brand by Frank Robinson. Fortunately, future managements stuck with it, as distinctive assets gather most of their power from consistent use and repetition. Or it may be purely abstract, such as the Nike 'swoosh', the origins of which are similarly casual. In 1971 Phil Knight of Blue Ribbon Shoes needed a design for a new running shoe, which he had not yet even decided to call 'Nike' – and he needed it in a hurry for a presentation to his Japanese investors. Still on the faculty of Portland State University, he paid a graphic design student called Carolyn Davidson $35 to draw something that 'suggested motion'. 'I don't love it', he said when she presented her work, 'but maybe it will grow on me.'

Or, as we've seen, a visual asset may become a character. The BBC's Children in Need appeal started in 1980, and for the first four years used a simple design of some children. In 1985 Joanna Lane, a young BBC designer, was asked to freshen the design. She felt that the appeal should be represented by a character, and thought of a teddy bear with a patch over its eye. No-one else was very enthusiastic, but she was allowed to carry on. Then, as Lane herself remembers it,

> 'I went to the production team and said, "we need to name it". So they turned around and said "if you think it's important to name him, you do it".

> 'It came from the heart – I looked to my own experience and named him in honour of my home town and my grandparents.'

Pudsey Bear is now one of the best known distinctive assets in British charity marketing, and over the years must have been worth many millions to the BBC appeal.

A brand name is itself a type of distinctive asset, and the difficulties of brand naming are actually much more to do with legal protection or unfortunate meanings in foreign languages than with finding 'just the right name' – and given that managers will think the choice of name so important, they are generally doomed to over-think it. We have seen how the name 'Quaker Oats' was simply derived from a trademark that Henry Crowell had acquired by chance, while nobody other than brand historians has ever known that the P.G. in P.G. Tips originally stood for 'Pre-Gestive' (an attempt to claim a benefit which had nothing whatever to do with the brand's later success).

Within some fairly broad limits, most brand names might as well be – and very often have been – quite arbitrary choices. Bailey's, the world leading brand of cream liqueur, was invented by a couple of consultants in 1970. Having had the idea for the product, they went out to buy some grouse in Soho, and walked past a restaurant called 'Bailey's Bistro'. One of them suggested they call the new drink 'Bailey's Irish Cream' – and the other agreed at once.

Also triggered by a chance event was Steve Jobs's choice of Apple for his new computer company:

> 'I was on one of my fruitarian diets. I had just come back from the apple farm. It sounded fun, spirited, and not intimidating. Apple took the edge off the word computer. Plus, it would get us ahead of Atari in the phone book.'

Apple was also a name that could easily be translated into a purely visual distinctive asset, as happened a little later when designer Ron Janoff came up with the now familiar outline of an apple (with a bite missing, just so it wouldn't be mistaken for a cherry).

If a good brand name ought to be more distinctive than descriptive, comparethemarket.com was not a great choice for a distinctive asset – until someone at their agency, VCCP in London, was amusing himself by reading the name out loud in a funny accent and realised it sounded like 'meerkat'. This had all the potential to create a highly distinctive asset, combining an integral link to the brand name with uniqueness, absurdity, and a visual image unlike anything else in that crowded category. (Oh, and it just happened to be another furry animal too.)

It's significant that so many stories like these, especially about the origins of names and logos, date from the early, entrepreneurial years of the brands, when one individual was both prepared and empowered to take what more bureaucratic managements would regard as crazy risks. Organisations like their decisions to be justifiable, based on evidence and logic, not on what you happened to pass on your way to work, the town your grandparents lived in, a local restaurant, or a ridiculous play on words. Organisations also like to contain their anxiety by commissioning expensive experts to design their assets, not the likes of Carolyn Davidson, Joanna Lane, Frank Robinson or Dorothy Ficken.

Yet both these habits encourage over-thinking and so often get in the way of creating a strong distinctive asset.

So as businesses become more mature, they are increasingly likely to take bad decisions about distinctive assets because they apply the wrong criteria. It is not just the apparently logical but mistaken quest for 'meaning' that leads them astray, but also a powerful cultural inhibition about looking silly. As Jenni Romaniuk observes, 'to not draw on the brand's rich history with a character, simply because of the risk of being perceived as "not serious", is a waste of a potentially valuable Distinctive Asset'.

This comment resonates with me, as I expect it will with others. During the 1990s I carried out a multi-country study into the Knorr brand, at that time owned by Best Foods. I remembered from my own childhood that packets of Knorr soup in the UK once carried pictures of a little pixie-like character called Knorrli, and researching through various historical reels I found a wonderful three minute cinema commercial (from 1951!) in which a stop-frame animated Knorrli went to an international market to buy produce from all over the world. The Knorr brand is especially strong in Switzerland, where it relaunched itself after the War (it originated in Germany), and Knorrli is a Swiss diminutive name – so when I visited the Swiss marketing department in the pretty village of Thayngen, near the German border, I was curious to know the story. I was told that Knorrli had been created just after the war, in a casual way that may now seem familiar to us – one of the management team drew a bowl of soup, added a smiley face to it, gave it a little body and a pointy hat, and that was it. I said I wondered why this rich heritage – which had even stuck in my own memory – was no longer to be seen in Switzerland or indeed anywhere else. They smiled at me. ' We thought it was time to grow up', they said: ' We are a serious food manufacturer, and Knorrli was just too childish'. (Today I notice that Knorrli has made a return on Knorr's Swiss website, though I suspect he's not being used to his full potential.)

But Knorrli's fate seems to have anticipated a more recent and quite marked trend in advertising, which is to avoid the use of characters at all. Orlando Wood identifies recurrent characters in advertising and recurrent scenarios attached to slogans as 'fluent devices'. He sees these as particularly powerful kinds of distinctive assets because, in addition to being fluently recognised and uniquely linked to the brand name, they are living, they create emotional response, and they connect with the right brain hemisphere. All these are conducive both to long term memory and to creating a rapid, emotionally based preference, using Kahneman's System 1 mode of thinking. We've already mentioned several examples of characters that are fluent devices – Honey Monster, the Cresta Bear, the Meerkats. Campaigns that rely on scenario-based fluent devices include the UK optician Specsavers ('Should've gone to Specsavers'), the Dutch insurance company, Centraal Beheer ('Just call us'), and, from the seventies, Heineken ('Refreshes the Parts that Other Beers Cannot Reach') .

It's clear that from very early on, characters, like slogans, have played an important part in many advertising campaigns: Phoebe Snow for the Lackawanna Railroad, Sunny Jim for Force, and Aunt Jemima for the eponymous pancake mix, all pre-dated TV by several decades. But they've often been hard to sell to clients who see them as childish, trivial, or vulgar. It once took us two years to persuade Quaker to run what proved to be a very successful campaign for granola bars which featured animated squirrels – the American marketing director once shouting at us, 'I am not having my company's fine products endorsed by a rodent!'.

But in the last couple of decades, it seems like agencies don't want to do them either. A series of analyses done by Orlando Wood proves that campaigns that use fluent devices are more effective than those that don't. But today, only 7% of campaigns in the UK and only 4% in the US *do* use character fluent devices. And taking the IPA Effectiveness Awards database, Wood shows that the proportion of entries using any fluent device has declined from 41% in 1992 to only 12% now.

Some of the arguments offered to justify this trend are almost certainly nonsense. There is no evidence that characters are somehow not relevant to millenials (as Jenni Romaniuk says, 'this seems a bit odd given the popularity of superhero movies!'). Another issue that's allowed to cloud the water is the move to digital media, which tends to use characters and all distinctive assets much less than other media. Yet Orlando Wood has carried out a comparative test of a British Gas digital ad with and without their character device of Wilbur the Penguin, and it shows that the version *with* the character performed better on reach, dwell time, and brand recall. There's actually a very strong argument that digital media require the use of distinctive assets/fluent devices even more than other media. And an equally strong, more general argument, that in an era where it's easier than ever to avoid ads, the only ones that will achieve anything are those that people find easy and attractive to process.

So why has the use of fluent devices and distinctive assets in advertising declined? For Wood, it's all part of a much wider, and very worrying, trend in society and culture as a whole – that we are increasingly operating under the dominance of the left brain hemisphere, which privileges logic, words, and abstract 'ideas about things' over the holistic, humanistic, ambiguous, interconnected pattern of 'things themselves' which the right brain experiences. In his book, *Lemon*, he illustrates this difference in two brilliant 'close readings' of a commercial from the 70s and another from the present day: the earlier, a famous ad for Heineken, uses narrative, character, interaction, humour, emotion, dialect, and cultural references to create an emotionally involving and memorable story (it's also based around a 'scenario' type fluent device), while the modern ad struggles to get attention by stylised posing, repetitive beats, and disconnected images behind words that dominate the screen.

It's a compelling and beautifully argued theory, founded in the extensive research of neuroscientist and psychologist Iain McGilchrist. And if we take into account that the right hemisphere of the brain is where we experience metaphor, humour and irony, poetry, idiom and music, it offers a profound, neuroscientifically based hypothesis as to why singing, showmanship, furry animals and all the rest of it have so often been used to engage with and influence people.

It may well be that the cultural shift we've seen in advertising reflects wider trends in the *zeitgeist*. But if we can also translate what's happened into a more industry-specific set of cultural behaviours and assumptions, we may give ourselves more room for hope that something can be done about it. There are fashions in all things, and to put it very simply, it seems that jingles, slogans and characters are all massively out of fashion in ad agencies at present. In Part Four, I shall consider how I think we got into this odd situation – and whether we can get out of it.

Before we go there, though, there is one more aspect of fame that deserves its own chapter. In this chapter and the previous two I've explored three of the four facets of fame – the need to reach mass audiences, the characteristics of what makes something sufficiently appealing or 'sticky', and the important role of distinctive assets. However, widespread and lasting fame is almost unimaginable without a fourth phenomenon coming into play, one that is of enormous benefit to celebrities and marketers alike. You can create the conditions for fame, with a compelling commercial, song, or film, powerful distinctive assets, and plenty of access to mass media; but it is what the public then does with it that will make the difference between a hit and a flop, a multi-million pound brand and an expensive failure. And while no-one can control what the public does, there are things that can make it easier for them to co-create fame and success.

Chapter Twelve
Infinitely Multiply

Extemplo Libyae magnas it Fama per urbes,
Fama, malum qua non aliud velocius ullum:
mobilitate viget viresque adquirit eundo…

AENEID IV, 173-5

Straightaway, Rumour travels through the great cities of Libya,
Rumour, than which no other evil is faster;
She thrives on her speed, and gains strength by going forward…

In Book IV of Virgil's epic poem, *The Aeneid*, Aeneas, fleeing the destruction of Troy, has landed at Carthage, where he has soon met and hooked up with the Queen, Dido. Like many modern celebrities, they don't want their affair to be public, but it seems they are powerless to stop the story getting out; and even in a mythical world long before paparazzi or tabloid newspapers, it's not long before everybody knows about it. Virgil's Latin word which I've translated as Rumour is *fama*, the direct ancestor of our English word, *fame*. *Fama* literally means something like 'what is said' – so it can also mean, depending on the context, public opinion, reputation, or renown. While in this passage it is described as an evil, (as rumour often is in its consequences), the word itself is deeply ambiguous – Latin authors sometimes writing of *bona fama* or *mala fama* ('a good or bad reputation') to make their meaning clear.

Virgil has embodied Fama as a sort of deity, a common poetic device, but his description of her tells us something quite accurate about how rumours actually spread – by a process which epidemiologists call *propagation*. Dido's kingdom presumably has no mass media, so the story reaches a wide audience without any broadcast events. It is significant, perhaps, that Virgil specifies how it travels through the 'cities' of Libya – as a citizen of Rome when it was already a city of over a million people, he would have personal experience of how quickly rumours can spread through a closely packed multitude. One person tells a group of friends, they each tell everyone they meet, and soon the result is exponential growth:

> She thrives on her speed, and gains strength by going forward.

So in its etymological origins, our word Fame describes, not something that is done *to* the public, but something the public create themselves through a systemic process. Nobody is in control of the process, which makes it easy to imagine 'Fama' as a being with a life of its own.

Three chapters ago, I was building a case that the creation of fame almost inevitably requires some mass communication events. Yet the original concept of 'fame' was very much based on word of mouth transmission, and it flourished as such for centuries before anything like our modern mass media existed. Is there a contradiction here?

I don't believe there is. We no longer live in the same world as Dido and Aeneas, or even Virgil. The Roman Empire had no mass media. But it was a highly literate and sophisticated society, whose network of interpersonal communications, even over long distances, has been seriously compared to modern social media. Widespread fame could therefore be created, despite the absence of mass communications, through word of mouth and written messages. The invention of printing, and subsequent developments such as the popular press, rapid travel, the telegraph, telephone, radio, cinema and television, all changed the rules of the fame game. The influence and the importance of mass media soon became inescapable: yet the effect of this change was not to reduce the importance of the networks of social interactions which preceded mass media, but paradoxically, if anything, to stimulate them further, by giving people so much more to talk about, argue about, endorse and buy into, share, wear, copy and create meaning from. Mass communications and social exchange are now interdependent parts of a single system, which is more complex than either.

So it is wrong to imagine that a single model from epidemiology can describe the way fame now spreads. We saw earlier that different diseases spread in radically different ways. Most viruses, for instance, are spread by *propagation* – one person passes the infection to two or more others, who in turn pass it on, and if this process is not interrupted it can rapidly become exponential, creating an epidemic or pandemic with massive consequences. On the other hand certain bacteria, such as cholera, are spread through *common source transmission*, such as a contaminated water supply. When Malcolm Gladwell asserted, rather too simplistically, that *'Ideas and products and messages and behaviours spread just like viruses do*,' he implied (intentionally or not) that they spread by propagation; conversely, when Derek Thompson chose to focus in *Hit Makers* on the story of the Broad Street Pump, he put his emphasis on common source transmission. But I suspect that when it comes to 'social contagion', it's not a question of one process or the other: both common source transmission *and* a version of propagation may be equally important.

Sociologists already recognise that social contagion is not exactly like biological contagion. 'If you get [a biological] infection, it will usually have come from a specific person', writes Adam Kucharski, author of *The Rules of Contagion*. 'Things aren't always so simple for social behaviour. We might only start doing something after we've seen multiple other people doing it... These behaviours are known as "complex contagions", because transmission requires multiple exposures.(p.105)' Kucharski's choice of words reminds us that social contagion does not only involve repeating the words of others; it is also, importantly, about how we copy their behaviours. As Mark Earls has also shown, we have a strong tendency to 'follow the herd', to do what we see many others doing. There are many reasons we do this, but the habit probably originated in some ancient principles of self preservation (if you see everyone else running away, you probably don't wait around, but join them). Many experiments have shown the power of our urge to conform to the behaviour of others: people will even sit in an increasingly smoke-filled room if surrounded by stooges who pretend nothing's wrong. And the potential for crowds, not just to conform to a norm, but to copy increasingly extreme behaviours can have deeply sinister consequences.

How does this tendency to copy others play out in the world of brands? We may choose to talk about our choice of computer, sportswear, coffee, or beer – or more often, we may not. But even when we don't, there are packaging and merchandise, designs, characters and logos which all clearly signal our choices – the Apple on the laptop, the Starbucks siren on the coffee cups in the meeting room, the Nike swoosh on our trainers. Never underestimate the power of both packaging and merchandise of all sorts in creating and maintaining the fame of both brands and celebrities. These are the visible, tangible tokens by which we are made aware of how popular anything is. The Jenny Lind cigar, the Sunny Jim doll, the classic Coke bottle on the café table, the red and white Marlboro pack (in the old days), the Abercrombie and Fitch sweatshirt, and the white earphones which I don't even need to name – these and a million other signals have long been our evidence for what everyone else is doing, and which we're therefore more inclined to want too.

*

To get an idea of the importance of such 'stuff' in the popularising of brands, fashions, and celebrities, you could do no better than visit The Museum of Brands.

Starting in his teens, Robert Opie has been throughout his life an avid – some might say obsessive – collector of ephemera. Perhaps it was something in his blood, as his parents, Iona and Peter Opie, were famous collectors of folklore, children's games and nursery rhymes. Opie began by collecting all the packaging he could find, fascinated by its colourful variety and social significance, and noticing that it almost invariably ended up in the bin; soon his scope extended to a wide range of branded cultural artefacts, including store displays, toys and games, books and music. The collection filled first his home, and then a series of warehouses: in 1984 he opened a museum in Gloucester Docks to display a selection. After this closed, he opened the Museum of Brands, now in its third and largest premises just outside Ladbroke Grove tube station in London.

The centrepiece of the permanent collection at the Museum of Brands is the Time Tunnel, 12,000 exhibits crowded into a sequence of floor to ceiling display cases which represent each decade from the late Victorian period to the present. Though this only shows about 3% of the total collection, the initial effect is bewildering, overwhelming – I have seen visitors wandering through it in a few minutes as if they don't know how to process this Aladdin's cave of packages, comics, magazines, plastic toys, board games, clothes, adverts and point of sale material, all luridly coloured and fighting for attention. But once you slow down and focus, it becomes endlessly fascinating – you can easily spend a couple of hours in the tunnel, and still feel you've only scratched the surface.

In some ways, my experiences in the Museum of Brands formed the genesis of this whole book. It's a wonderful corrective to our modern ideas that brands are fundamentally about abstract values or higher purposes, because it shows at every step of the way how they build their actual existence in tangible, everyday items and in popular culture. And I mean, *popular*. One thing that struck me forcibly as I walked through the Time Tunnel was that, while fashions, fonts, and styles of art direction change from one decade to the next, the fundamental themes of what people like best *en masse* remain pretty much the same: from the 1880s to the present day, I dare to suggest, nearly all the exhibits could be put into one or more of the following general categories:

- Celebrities – singers, actors, film stars, comedians, presenters, famous people of all sorts
- Cartoon characters, with anthropomorphised animals perennially popular
- Popular Music and musicians
- Films, radio and TV Series (and latterly, computer games)
- Pretty girls
- Cute kids, kittens, puppies, etc
- Sports and games and sporting heroes
- Children's toys
- Topical news of the day (with a special section for 'patriotism in time of war')

- Latest developments in technology and 'the future' (from crystal sets and horseless carriages to space travel and fitness apps)
- Nostalgia and imaginary rural Edens.

It is hard to remain so enthusiastic about the theology of the brand onion when you are looking at a packet of Instant Whip with Fred Flintstone on it, or a box of biscuits featuring Pip, Squeak and Wilfred. It is in this realm of the tangible and specific, and (by some judgements) the ephemeral, the clichéd and the vulgar, that most marketing has done its effective work throughout the past century and a half.

The packs, pictures, toys, clothes, games and magazines we see in the Museum of Brands may appear trivial and disposable, but they were all of value to people at one time – of enough value, at least, that people wanted to buy them, own them, display them, wear them, or give them as Christmas presents. They had meaning for people in the context of their lives. That's why, quite apart from any professional interest we may have in the history of publicity, the experience of walking through the Time Tunnel can be an emotional one, and this is an important aspect of its appeal to the public at large. We can laugh at this huge collection of ephemeral tat – that's also part of the pleasure of visiting the Museum – but let's also remember what these things may have meant to the people who had them in their lives (and sometimes, those people include us).

This was brought home to me, as things sometimes are, by a fictional example. In the 'Nausicaa' episode of James Joyce's *Ulysses*, Gerty MacDowell, an unmarried woman in her early twenties, sits on the beach at Sandymount in the gathering summer dusk, while her girl friends, Edy and Cissy, play nearby with Edy's baby brothers. In a typical 'stream of consciousness' Joyce's prose modulates seamlessly and wickedly between a parody of the romantic fiction that Gerty loves, the archly euphemistic language of this 'respectable' southern suburb of Dublin, and Gerty's own fantasies:

> Everyone thought the world of her for her gentle ways. It was Gerty who turned off the gas at the main every night and it was Gerty who tacked up on the wall of that place where she never forgot every fortnight the chlorate of lime Mr Tunney the grocer's Christmas almanac the picture of halcyon

days where a young gentleman in the costume they used to wear then with a threecornered hat was offering a bunch of flowers to his ladylove with oldtime chivalry through her lattice window. You could see there was a story behind it. The colours were done something lovely. She was in a soft clinging white in a studied attitude and the gentleman was in chocolate and he looked a thorough aristocrat. She often looked at them dreamily when there for a certain purpose and felt her own arms that were white and soft just like hers with the sleeves back and thought about those times…

Ulysses is set in 1904, and by then the practice of offering coloured prints as promotional items had been increasingly popular for at least twenty years. The first really famous example was probably Millais's painting, 'Bubbles', which was bought by Thomas Barrett to use as an advertisement for Pears Soap. It was so popular that he made it available as a coloured postcard, a black and white engraving, and as a jigsaw puzzle. Barrett's great rival, William Lever of Sunlight Soap, retaliated by buying William Powell Frith's painting, 'The New Frock', from the Royal Academy. It showed a little girl proudly holding up her new white pinafore, which Frith had meant to convey a moral about vanity. When Lever, without warning, reissued the picture as an advertisement by adding the caption 'So Clean', Frith was so angry that he took him to court. Lever happily accepted this as just more publicity for his brand.

We can sneer, as Joyce I think does, at Gerty MacDowell and her romantic fantasies around this cheesy picture, which has been given away as a promotion by the local grocer and lovingly pinned up in the outside loo. 'Halcyon Days' is kitschy, low culture (I don't know if Joyce had an actual picture in mind, but it sounds very like something by Federico Andreotti, or maybe Marcus Stone or Edouard Toudouze). And it's further tarnished by its use as advertising. But we can also see that it means an awful lot to Gerty; it's both a thing of beauty for her ('the colours were done something lovely'), and a reflection of her own dreams of love and romance – dreams which we later learn are unlikely to become reality, because Gerty is disabled in an age when this was likely to be an insuperable barrier to marriage. It's a reminder that for the great majority of ordinary people at this time, a quality coloured print could be something highly valued.

Mr Tunney's chromolithographic print of 'Halcyon Days' is an early example of what we now call 'branded content', and it illustrates the timeless principle that people will value, keep, display or share branded material, not because it 'sells' to them, but because it offers them something of value: a travelling show, an attractive decoration for the home, or a sixty second comedy starring Rowan Atkinson. Faris Yakob tried to define our modern use of the word 'content' in 2015, when it was still relatively novel:

> Personally, I feel brand content, as we are using the term, is *something created by / for a brand that people choose to consume* – as opposed to advertising which we essentially pay people to consume, indirectly.

I can go along with the first part of this sentence, but I don't accept the distinction between 'content' and 'advertising' – in my view, much of the best advertising has been precisely 'something created by / for a brand that people choose to consume'. Some of this has appeared in paid-for media, while much has come in the form of merchandise, events, and other things. In either case, for people to become an active part of the creation of fame, they need to be given things that they 'choose to consume': a catch phrase, a character, a competition, a cause, a calendar, a cuddly toy.

*

So we copy what we see others do, and we are also influenced by the things we see them own and use and value. But what we've been calling 'social contagion' involves much more than just imitation. We don't just copy others – we also interact with them, we are emotionally influenced by them, we get satisfactions from talking about things we have in common, or arguing about things we differ over, we act things out, we form tribes and alliances and rivalries, we make collective meanings, rules, and customs, which shape our experience and our behaviour. Our role in a biological contagion is fundamentally passive – we either allow the organism to infect us, or we manage to avoid it or mitigate it in some way. But in social contagion we are also active agents, both as individuals and, perhaps more importantly, as aggregations of individuals.

People didn't just passively absorb 'Rock Around the Clock' as if it were a bacterium – they made it into something new, which formed a large part of what was then 'passed on' to others, and which was then amplified by the media. 'Rock Around the Clock' may have needed the 'common source' of *The Blackboard Jungle* to trigger its success, but the effect of this broadcast event was not simply to 'infect' millions of individual teenagers, but to stimulate them to copy each other, to use the song to invent new forms of interaction, to collectively create social meanings and pleasures and behaviours around the song that were not intrinsic to the song itself. And these behaviours in turn generated vastly more media coverage, which broadcast it back to them and to the wider public. Exactly as *The Times* wrote in 1869, explaining how Barnum had created 'Lindomania',

> This *furore* once excited, was chronicled by the newspapers, and thus infinitely multiplied, as heat and light are increased by being reflected.

Once again we notice the interaction of broadcast or common source transmission, and propagation by conversation and imitation among the public. Barnum understood from the outset not just how to work the media, and how to work the crowd; he also understood how to use the media to influence the crowd, and the crowd to influence the media. Without the participation of the public – the crowds, the riots, the auctions, the buying of merchandise, and so on – there would have been little incentive for the media to take such a sustained and intense interest in the Jenny Lind tour as they did. And without the media – the headline coverage, the satirical cartoons, the gossip and the controversy – the topic would soon have faded from the public mind.

Throughout his career, Barnum used a wide range of techniques for exciting public involvement in his projects, and probably all of these have been familiar tools of publicists ever since. The creation of events and exhibitions which would gather physical crowds, from his museums to his later great circus; the stimulation of controversy and argument (he was even known to suggest to visitors that the blue whale skeleton in his museum, which was entirely genuine, was in fact a fake); competitions, like his infamous 'baby contests', in which the public would act both as participants and as rival factions of supporters; and, of course, the sale and distribution of merchandise which would enable as many people as possible to 'own' an aspect of what he was promoting, and which 'infinitely multiplied' its ubiquity and mental availability. All of these actions were both encouraged and supported by the media, and provided material for the media to respond to and broadcast further.

Let's consider one example of the creative and improvisatory talent with which Barnum involved and excited the public. Early in his career, when he was still only 25 years old and relatively unknown, he came across an Italian juggler and 'professor of equilibrium and plate dancing' who called himself 'Signor Antonio'. According to A.H. Saxon's monumental life of Barnum,

> Antonio's great speciality was his ability to make dinner plates, washbowls, and other species of crockery 'jump, fly, and dance quadrilles, minuets, waltzes, and contra dances' in time to music on the end of sticks and swords, which he either held in his hands or balanced – sometimes with other objects such as forks interposed – on his nose and chin. He could keep as many as ten plates spinning at once; and his other feats included hopping about the stage on a single stilt while firing a musket at a target (p.77).

Barnum engaged Antonio for a year, changed his name to the more memorable 'Signor Vivalla', and began exhibiting his skills at the Franklin Theatre in New York. Promoting the 'professor of equilibrium' energetically via the newspapers, Barnum took his protégé on tour through several other cities, with great success – until the show reached Philadelphia, where, for the first time, Vivalla was hissed by the audience. It turned out some of the spectators were already loyal supporters of their own local circus juggler, one J.B. Roberts, and resented an outsider appearing on his home turf.

Barnum at once placed advertisements in the next day's papers, in which he offered a challenge: $1,000 for anyone else who could replicate Vivalla's feats. Roberts publicly accepted the challenge, before realising, too late, that at such short notice he could not possibly copy everything that Vivalla did (the condition for the prize). He was about to walk away in anger when Barnum made him an offer, which had been his real plan all along: if Roberts would appear on stage in the promised duel of skills with Vivalla, he would be paid $30 a night. Roberts, being short of engagements, was happy to accept, and Barnum set to work to inflame the audience's sense of rivalry between their local man and the foreign pretender. To return to Saxon's account,

> By the time the contest came off before a crowded house... Vivalla and Roberts had been thoroughly rehearsed in their parts, thereby ensuring a suspenseful performance that lasted about sixty minutes... At the end of the contest the two jugglers, glaring daggers at each other, appeared before the curtain, and Roberts revealed he had been labouring under the handicap of a sprained wrist. He now delivered a fiery challenge of his own; if Vivalla could duplicate all of *his* feats on some future night, he would willingly forfeit $500. The challenge was immediately accepted, of course; and while the audience out front was in an uproar, the two bitter rivals were laughing and shaking hands on the other side of the curtain...(p.78)

In this way Barnum, who had already engaged Roberts for another month, created the basis for an even more successful series of shows.

Barnum had not, of course, invented the idea of the public contest, which probably counts as one of the most ancient forms of entertainment; he simply had the imagination to apply it to a situation which others might have seen as a setback rather than an opportunity. A contest of any kind seems to have a perennial appeal, not just because it creates a continually new narrative whose outcome is unknown, but because of all the incidental pleasures it allows the spectators – supporting or detracting the contestants, analysing their actions and their characters in debate or argument. While boxing or wrestling matches and sporting contests of all sorts never go out of fashion, and talent contests have been a regular winner for generations, recent decades have seen the format extended into a huge variety of unlikely activities in the form of reality TV shows: cake baking, pottery, sewing, entrepreneurialism, or just the ability to survive in a particular social environment as in *Big Brother* or *Love Island*.

Who would have anticipated that ballroom dancing could become the subject of a top rating TV show across the world? Yet *Strictly Come Dancing/ Dancing With The Stars* maintains its massive level of fame because it combines a contest format, enhanced by weekly public voting, with the personal relations and sexual frissons created by the close physical collaboration of the dance partners, and these together stimulate lively conversations among both public and media about what is happening both on and off screen, as these typical headlines suggest:

Stacey: 'Why Kevin and I didn't think we had a chance to win'
Strictly Stars: We are sorry for drunken snog
Strictly X-rated! Dance stars' secret fling is leaked on the net!

With the leaked rumour of a 'secret fling' – a subject of perennial fascination since the time of Dido and Aeneas, it seems – perhaps this chapter has come full circle. Fame still has its roots in *fama* – what people want to talk about, share with each other and become a part of. And what that is can be seeded, provoked and stimulated in many ways – through broadcasts, merchandise, signs and signals, the encouragement of controversy – but it can never ultimately be controlled. Fame only really 'gains strength by going forward' once the public takes an active part in its creation. And people will only do that if enough of them get some kind of pleasure or satisfaction from doing so.

*

In these four chapters, I have suggested that widespread and lasting fame, whether for entertainers, celebrities, or commercial brands, almost invariably depends on meeting four conditions.

- First, whatever is offered must be sufficiently interesting or appealing to people;

- Secondly, it must find ways to reach mass audiences;

- Thirdly it must be distinctive, unique and memorable (and it helps a lot if it's legally ownable too);

- Fourthly, the public and the media themselves must engage with it actively (and they can be encouraged though not compelled to do so).

These propositions may sound obvious, even banal. But let's consider also what they leave out as relatively unimportant. Fame does not, for instance, automatically reward the best product or performer – unless they can fulfil these other conditions, they won't be famous. And that's unlikely to happen by pure chance, though very occasionally it does. Fame does not require any meaningful kind of differentiation, nor of originality: something that is largely familiar or which conforms to category norms may be just as successful in the fame stakes, and sometimes may do better than something that's just too novel or too weird. And fame can never be entirely predicted or controlled, because it emerges from a complex system of interactions; however, the chances of it happening can be increased from very low to somewhat more likely by those who pay conscious attention to nurturing these four conditions in any way they can.

So why, in that case, does the advertising industry today so often seem to ignore these simple principles – even to consciously avoid them? With a dwindling number of honourable exceptions, it seems to me that professional practice in the twenty-first century is dominated by the following characteristics:

- An obsession with targeting and efficiency, and too much wishful thinking about the power of virality, both routinely eclipse any ambition to achieve mass coverage.

- Far too much of what is produced by ad agencies not only lacks any popular appeal, but seems proud of the fact that it has avoided it. 'Popular' is almost a term of abuse.

- The use of 'distinctive assets', as was shown earlier, has declined almost to the point of extinction – just at the moment when we seem to have a better scientific basis for understanding why they matter so much.

- And in the absence of these first three conditions, it is not surprising if most brands form a very small part of today's public conversations.

In the concluding section of this book, I would like to offer some suggestions as to how we got into this extraordinary situation – and how we could make advertising popular and effective again.

Part Four

What Kind of Creativity Do We Need?

I fear all the sins we may commit in the name of 'Creativity'. I fear that we may be entering an age of phonies.

BILL BERNBACH

The creative man is obsessed not with real people and their wants and desires, but with creativity as an end in itself. And since nobody can tell him what creativity is, he is forced to conclude that it is anything that wins the Grand Prix de L'Arc de Triomphe at the Wexford Film Festival.

JEREMY BULLMORE

The rage for creativity… came quickly to mean an appeal to nonconformist rebellion…

THOMAS FRANK, *THE CONQUEST OF COOL*

What if the change the industry really needs is to refocus itself towards producing the kind of brilliant, insightful, creative advertising that will get noticed and remembered by consumers?

EAON PRITCHARD, *WHERE DID IT ALL GO WRONG?*

Chapter Thirteen

The C Word

I don't know if you've noticed, but up to this point in the book – apart from one quote from Bill Bernbach, and in one later comment on that quote – I have not used the word *creativity*.

My avoidance of the term was deliberate, but I didn't find it difficult. On the few occasions when I was briefly tempted to use the word, a moment's reflection showed that I could make my meaning clearer and more precise by writing something else.

It's possible that some of my readers have been mentally filling the word in anyway. Such a reader, if I've made my intentions at all plain, might even now be paraphrasing the main argument of the book something like this:

> 'You build a case that much advertising is simply more effective when it is entertaining, emotionally moving or otherwise involving; that it should make frequent use of music, humour, spectacle, song and dance; that it can be playful, even childish, and should not disdain to use cartoons or talking animals; that all these things create mental availability, liking for a brand, and help to build powerful distinctive assets.

'In short, you are arguing – as agencies always do – for more *creativity* in advertising. The best agencies, of course – the *creative* agencies – have always tried to do this, but have continually been thwarted by their clients who want every ad to be a boring rehearsal of sales arguments. Creativity is the magic ingredient that we know how to make, but not enough clients will buy it – especially today.'

The first of these paragraphs would be a good summary of what I have been trying to show. But the second paragraph is not really what I meant at all.

If only it were so simple! Of course, if the word 'creativity' clearly meant all the things in the first paragraph, it would not be too bad. But today it emphatically doesn't – and I'm not sure that it ever entirely did.

Can we even say what it does mean?

When I worked at BMP in the seventies and eighties, we would have described ourselves without hesitation as a creative agency, and acknowledged 'creativity' as our core value (if we had used that sort of talk in those days). We also produced work that was universally popular, and which ticked all the boxes in that first paragraph above. The same would have been true of our great rivals, Collett Dickenson Pearce. CDP was radically different from BMP; while we insisted on the value of research to ensure our work was popular, they rejected it as a constraint, and based decisions entirely on judgement. But looking back on it all now, I suspect we each did equally well in creating famous, popular, long-lasting and effective campaigns. We did Courage and John Smiths, they did Heineken; we did the Smash Martians, and they did Hovis; we did Hellmann's Mayonnaise and Kia-Ora, while they did Parker Pens and Benson and Hedges. We differed in how we went about it, but we tacitly shared a common vision of the sort of work we wanted to make, and for the most part we both achieved it.

But there were other agencies in London who produced popular, entertaining campaigns which no-one in the business regarded as 'creative', and which rarely, if ever, won the creative awards which we so prized. I'm thinking of an agency like Allen, Brady and Marsh, whose flamboyant Chairman, Peter Marsh, had begun his career in the theatre and found his way to advertising by way of TV.

The products of his agency were shamelessly showbusiness, catchy slogans and jingles delivered with a maximum of razzmatazz. All of this we and CDP sneered at, along with Marsh's white suits and Rolls-Royces. It was popular, it was successful, and ABM's campaigns for British Rail, Harp Lager, Midland Bank, Woolworth's, Weetabix, and Guinness are probably as fondly remembered among those of a certain age as any of ours. But, somehow, it was not 'creative'.

It seems that by the 1970s the word 'creativity' as used in advertising had already come to mean something other than merely popular or entertaining, though it still often embraced those qualities as well. With the passing of time this would become less and less true, and the terms almost mutually exclusive. How did this come to be?

There's a turning point somewhere around 1960 when the ad business, having been torn between its undeniable roots in the popular culture of the travelling show and its aspirations to be professional, managerial, and rational, suddenly discovered a third narrative that apparently offered a way out – advertising could be hip. Ads could be knowing, self-referential, tongue-in-cheek, and the creators of advertising could reinvent themselves as rebels whose raison d'etre was to fight the corporate dullness of their clients. The story of this strange metamorphosis, which still configures so much of agency culture today, is brilliantly told by sociologist Thomas Frank in his 1997 book *The Conquest of Cool*. Doyle Dane Bernbach led the way, firmly rejecting both rules and research and producing a series of high profile campaigns which were witty, stylish, and iconoclastic – campaigns which were not just entertaining and distinctive, but, unlike nearly all previous advertising, cool enough to be admired by metropolitan hipsters, and even by advocates of the counter-culture. The Volkswagen campaign especially epitomised this, as the car itself was deliberately presented as an icon of alternative values, of economy and ecology versus status and conformity.

Bill Bernbach was closely followed by other high-profile figures such as George Lois, Mary Wells, Howard Gossage, Jerry Della Femina, and Carl Ally. The collective influence of these powerful personalities was vastly disproportionate to their small agencies and mostly small-budget clients (Gossage's beautiful and much admired ads nearly all appeared nowhere except the *New Yorker*). Between them, they established 'creativity' as a rallying cry for turning everything about the boring old ad business on its head – including, though they didn't always make it explicit, the idea that its productions should appeal to the masses. As Thomas Frank puts it,

> Just as academics were coming round to the forbidden joys of popular culture, leading admen were learning to shun them (p.76).

Bill Bernbach's agency was itself counter-cultural, Jewish-led in an era when the ad business was predominantly WASP, and developed a reputation for refusing to do clients' bidding in a culture of yes-men. Following this distinctive path, DDB became successful (at one time, No 3 in the US), admired and envied in the business – and above all, cool. And no-one did more to celebrate and popularise that recent neologism, 'creativity', than Bernbach himself:

> Is creativity some obscure, esoteric art form? Not on your life. It's the most practical thing a businessman can employ.

By contrast, David Ogilvy never had a good thing to say about the C-word. He called it 'a high-falutin term for the work I have to do between now and next Tuesday'. As late as the 1980s, he could point out, correctly, that the word wasn't even in the Oxford English Dictionary. (It is now, along with *twerking* and *yarn-bombing*.)

So when Bernbach's many disciples wanted to know what 'creativity' actually looked like, they naturally fixated on one particular set of models – the ads that DDB had produced in the sixties. Not that there was anything wrong with these much-praised ads in themselves. But they were only one rather narrow type of ad, written for a largely middle-class, metropolitan audience, and deliberately eschewing many of the techniques that made other campaigns more massively famous and memorable. DDB were unbeatable on a certain type of sophisticated wit, but seldom if ever created characters or other distinctive brand assets, seldom if ever used songs or sentiment. I don't think that during Bill Bernbach's lifetime his agency ever produced a Jolly Green Giant or a Pillsbury Doughboy, a Pepperidge Farm wagon or a Ronald McDonald , a Coke 'Hilltop' or a Hovis 'Bicycle', a PG Chimps or a Honey Monster. All this sort of thing was not cool – and so not considered creative.

Far from liberating the ad industry to a new age of popular carnival, Bernbach's unintended legacy was to reinforce in a different way the entrenched belief that the world of popular culture and mass entertainment was distinctly beneath the high calling of the advertising profession. Instead of aspiring to science and professionalism, it embraced another kind of ambition – to produce stuff that was cool enough to appeal to your friends in Manhattan, San Francisco, or Hampstead.

And while rules and research in advertising both have many limitations, Bernbach's absolute rejection of both legitimised a lack of interest in the responses of the wider public. This disconnection became an act of faith in the agencies that followed DDB, leaving them free to define 'creativity' as whatever they wanted it to be, and certainly nothing to do with popular appeal. Creativity might mean trying to do ads that looked like DDB's, or it might mean simply doing the reverse of whatever had been done in the past. There is a big difference between a healthy scepticism about rules, and a conviction that you must always do the precise opposite. Breaking rules quickly becomes a rule in itself, as Thomas Frank pointed out:

> By the mid 1960s the anti-principles of creativity had become rule book stuff
> in their own right. In a 1966 handbook for copywriters, a Y&R creative leader
> instructs readers that 'The first rule for copywriters is to be suspicious of rules.
> Rules have a way of turning into ruts' (p.92).

By an extension of the same principle, the meaning of 'creativity' was soon ruled un-discussable. Rosser Reeves, at his induction into the 'Copywriters' Hall of Fame' in 1965, truculently challenged the award sponsors, the Advertising Writers' Association of New York (AWANY), to define 'creativity'. Their response was that: 'AWANY must, by its nature, come out against any formulas for advertising'. In other words, creativity was officially defined as indefinable.

That lack of definition soon became a standing joke. Yet the void labelled 'creativity' was soon to be filled in practice with something very specific. Jeremy Bullmore, the creative director of J. Walter Thompson during the long period when it was the largest agency in London, and responsible for many popular and famous campaigns, made a serious point in a light-hearted way at the inaugural conference of the Account Planning Group in 1978:

The creative man is obsessed not with real people and their wants and desires, but with creativity as an end in itself. And since nobody can tell him what creativity is, he is forced to conclude that it is anything that wins the Grand Prix de L'Arc de Triomphe at the Wexford Film Festival.

This last flourish was actually a humorous code for 'the Palme d'Or at the Cannes Advertising Film Festival', a prize which had taken on ever greater significance during the seventies. The first *Festival Internationale du Film Publicitaire* was held in Venice in September 1954 . This was before commercial television had even started in the UK, and long before it was allowed in France (1968); the Screen Advertising World Association intended it to promote advertising in cinemas, modelling it on the Cannes Film Festival which had been going since the late forties. The winning films from the early years, which I can no longer find on YouTube, were weird, exotic, parodic, fond of animation techniques, and, unconstrained by the discipline of the thirty second TV ad, usually three minutes long. I have been unable to discover whether any of them were considered commercially effective, or indeed how far they achieved public exposure at all.

But by the 1970s the Festival, which alternated between Cannes and Venice until 1983, had become by general consent the most highly regarded award for TV advertising in the world. (It didn't at this stage include media other than film, though there were other prestigious awards that did, led by Britain's D&AD, which began in 1963.) With the advent of colour TV in the UK at the beginning of the seventies, London agencies nurtured a new generation of commercial directors who transformed the genre, such as Ridley Scott, Hugh Hudson, and Alan Parker. As a result British commercials began to win big at Cannes and Venice: in 1976 Britain got 10 of 19 Gold Lions, plus the Palme d'Or.

Understandably, British agencies were over the moon, and creative awards became increasingly important signals of success for them and especially for the art directors and copywriters themselves. But there was a danger here too, which Jeremy Bullmore had gently hinted at in his 1978 speech. Later, he would be more explicit:

> The backlash to the creative awards was that people in agencies were losing their compass bearings, and doing work just designed to win awards.

From their origins, all creative awards have always been prizes for craft and artistry, not for effectiveness or commercial outcomes. So there was always the worry that 'work designed to win awards' would not necessarily be what worked best for the client, and that the perception of this could reduce clients' confidence in their agencies. (This was one argument for the creation of the IPA Effectiveness Awards in 1980.) But, on the whole, throughout the seventies and eighties, and even to some extent later, creative awards still mainly went to ads that were popular, and so presumably, often effective – even though many other highly successful and popular campaigns were never going to win the very specific type of recognition that creative awards juries gave. The Gold TV campaigns in that *annus mirabilis* of 1976, for example, included the Ty-Phoo Gnu, by Geers Gross; the Tic-Tac detective, by BMP; and the Hovis 'Boy on a Bike' by CDP. All the winning work was popular and famous, as well as being beautifully crafted.

This degree of overlap between popularity and awards disguised the insidious way in which creative awards would increasingly come to dominate agency practice. In the seventies and eighties, awards may have been innocent enough celebrations of well-crafted or entertaining ads, but by the nineties they were becoming an end in themselves, in ways which had damaging consequences for agencies – and more so for their clients. During this period I remember that my own agency's global management set each local office two targets, with real penalties if they were not met: one, predictably, was financial, but the other was to win a certain number of specified awards. Our London office was therefore compelled to do whatever it could to meet the awards target, and it achieved this over a number of years almost entirely on just two accounts. One was Volkswagen, which I suspect continued to attract awards as much because of tradition as anything else (and during this time the ads, once so charming and clever and witty, seemed to me to become more and more weird, threatening, and unpleasant – 'edginess' being increasingly a quality that awards juries were known to favour. If you don't believe me, search on YouTube for 'VW Lupo commercial 2003'.) The other account was an upscale London store called Harvey Nichols, whose tiny budget must have made an insignificant contribution to the vast amount of creative time and talent that was invested in it so that, year after year, each new set of arch, oh-so-clever ads could garner its gongs.

The obsession with awards created other distortions. Creative staff who won big awards could, like sporting superstars, expect ever greater salaries and job offers from other agencies. While creative teams fought each other to work on the two accounts where they could win fame and corresponding fortune, it became increasingly difficult to motivate them to spend much energy on anything else. As creative awards are always given to named individuals, there was a serious disincentive to teamwork, and a stimulus to the most bitter rivalry. And even to have a conversation with a creative team about how the public (as opposed to a jury) might respond to their work, never the easiest thing, became increasingly impossible.

As the nineties passed into the noughties, BMP/DDB London felt more and more like a two speed agency. After the box marked 'creativity' was ticked off each year by winning our quota of awards on the same two accounts, the ambition to produce exciting or attractive work on all the others dwindled. Big international accounts, in particular, produced work of increasing dullness, but were essential in order to meet our financial targets (and to cover the considerable costs of winning awards, whose entry fees alone became eye-wateringly large).

By the time I left the agency in 2005, I felt that more and more of the work we produced was neither effective, nor – as it had once been – entertaining and popular. And yet, each year, we were told with more and more self-congratulation that our agency's guiding value, its one, non-negotiable commitment as proven by our awards record, was 'creativity'.

Since then it seems things have continued to get worse, across the industry. As copywriter Steve Harrison argues in his brilliant 2020 polemic, *Can't Sell, Won't Sell*, creative awards in the past decade have increasingly become dominated by fashionable fantasies of social purpose, rather than commerce, or even art – today's version of 'the conquest of cool'. Perhaps related to this trend, an analysis by Peter Field in 2019 of the IPA Effectiveness Awards database shows that creatively awarded campaigns which also won effectiveness awards used to be several times more efficient than non-awarded campaigns. But the last ten years have seen what Field calls 'a *catastrophic* decline in the typical efficiency multiplier achieved by creatively awarded campaigns', so that now they are no better than others.

For all my serious reservations, I am not against creative awards. Over the whole course of their history I suspect they have encouraged much more good work than bad. They ought to be a valuable celebration of craft, imagination, and many things about ads that serve to create fame, liking and distinctiveness. But they have gradually lost touch with what matters most in advertising, which is popularity and fame, and have so contributed to today's crisis of creativity. I would love to see them play a part in resolving that crisis.

But an unhealthy obsession with creative awards is only one aspect of what's gone wrong with our ideas of creativity.

Chapter Fourteen

Blowing Shit Up

Today, the Cult of Creativity continues to grow. The Cannes Festival changed its name some years ago to the 'Festival of Creativity', expanding its scope beyond traditional definitions of advertising, and enabling it to multiply further the numbers of categories for entries. It is now a big business in its own right, and although there were many times in the past when Cannes was considered a bit of a boondoggle for art directors and a throwback to the era of Mad Men extravagance, *everyone* now goes there – the clients, the big agency holding companies, and, dominating the seafront, the social media and ad tech companies.

In 2015, even I went. I remember standing in a long queue in the blazing sun to register at the Palais des Festivals, a massive, irregularly shaped building, with a grand flight of steps designed for film stars' entrances and exits. Above us, a huge electronic display twinkled in the bright sun, bombarding us with words on the theme of 'creativity' (not images, just words, all in upper case): MAGIC, INNOVATION, DARING, ENERGY, GENIUS, TALENT, BRAVERY, DETERMINATION, PUSHING BOUNDARIES, NEVER GIVE UP. The words combined to suggest that creativity in advertising requires both some indefinable quality of genius and an obsessive, self-denying capacity for endurance. There was also a clear undertone of anger or rebellion – echoed by other posters inside the Palais with lines like 'How to Blow Shit Up', 'Break the System', and 'Creativity is the only way to Survive', this last word rendered in letters of dripping blood. It made 'creativity' sound like a life and death struggle, or a violent revolution. As I sweltered in the queue and wished I'd brought a hat, I reflected on what other words might have been here, but weren't: DREAMING, REFLECTION, CONVERSATION, IDLENESS, PLAYFULNESS, HAVING FUN, GETTING LOST, FOOLING AROUND… or then again, PRACTICE, TECHNIQUE, CRAFT, ARTISTRY, TASTE, FEELING, TRADITION, ENCHANTMENT. When I finally got inside the Palais, I saw a poster about a well-intentioned project to increase gender diversity in advertising creative departments – only 11% of Creative Directors are currently women – which cited 'feminine' values such as *empathy, intuition, collaboration*. But these words were not on the front of the Palais.

I have learnt from working with discourse analyst Gill Ereaut that the language used in organisations is a powerful aspect of their enduring cultures, and I therefore believe the male domination of creative departments and the nature of the words used about 'creativity' are not unconnected. Soon after my trip to Cannes, I visited one of London's most creatively awarded agencies. The first thing that caught my eye in their smart offices was a reception desk about twenty feet long, covered in a torrent of writing, all (again) in upper case, and reversed out of black (just to annoy the ghost of David Ogilvy?). I'll quote, I admit just a little selectively, from this, but I'm aiming to capture what seems to me its distinctive flavour – the original is about five times longer:

DOES IT ZAG? IS IT ORIGINAL? IS IT TRUE? DOES IT STAND OUT LIKE THE DOG'S PROVERBIALS? …HAS IT MADE THAT LEAP FROM GOOD TO GREAT? ARE YOU EXCITED BY IT? DOES IT FEEL FRESH? RARE? BLOODY? DOES IT KICK STATUS QUO IN THE TEETH, HOOF CONVENTION IN THE NADS & POKE ORDINARY SHARPLY IN BOTH EYES?… CAN IT LIVE,BREATHE AND KICK ASS IN EVERY CHANNEL? …IS IT A LITTLE SCARY? WILL IT MAKE ANYONE SAY –F*#K I WISH I'D DONE THAT!? … WHEN THE REST OF THE WORLD ZIGS, DOES IT ZAG?

I could not mistake the relentless aggression of the metaphors, the juvenile machismo of the language. And as in Cannes, once I started noticing it, I realised that it has come to pervade much of the discourse of ad agency creative departments in one way or another. The central image or metaphor for creativity is destruction, rebellion, violence – the poke in the eye, the kick in the teeth. One major agency, TBWA, has for some decades now built its reputation on the theme of 'Disruption'. Sir John Hegarty has written, as if it were something obvious, that

> Creativity is, after all, about *breaking something down* and putting something new in its place. (*emphasis added*)

Paul Arden, the late creative director and author of a best-selling little book called *It's Not How Good You Are, It's How Good You Want To Be*, wrote,

> All creative people need something to rebel against.

Yet every example I have given earlier in this book – such as Barclaycard, 'Hilltop', or the Honey Monster – suggests that all this is, at best, one small strand in the process of creating something that appeals to the public or has any lasting value. Familiarity is as important as originality; craft is much more important than destruction; playfulness, collaboration, and patience (however painful) are normally much more productive than anger and machismo. It's not just about blowing shit up.

The gender bias in today's creative departments is all the more striking because historically, in the days when most departments in most agencies were still staffed exclusively by men, the one role where a woman could realistically apply for a job was as a copywriter. The logic for this seemed to be that (a) women were at least expected to be good at stringing words together (look at Jane Austen, or Agatha Christie!) and (b) because many of the products advertised were bought by women, so other women would know best how to talk to them. In the 1920s, Dorothy L. Sayers worked as a copywriter at the London agency, Bensons, gaining in the process much useful material for a Lord Peter Wimsey mystery, *Murder Must Advertise*. During the same period the head of copy at J. Walter Thompson in New York was Helen Lansdowne Resor, whom David

Ogilvy called 'the greatest copywriter of her generation', and who employed many female copywriters. Many famous campaigns of the fifties and sixties were written by women, such as Shirley Polykoff's 'Does She... or Doesn't She?' for Clairol at FCB, and Mary Fillius's 'I dreamt I was...' for Maidenform. Perhaps most ironically, the first 'creative department' – formed by Bill Bernbach when he merged the previously separate realms of copywriting and art direction – contained a high proportion of women. Head of Copy throughout the glory years of DDB was Phyllis Robinson, whom Bernbach had worked with at Grey. Judy Protas wrote 'You don't have to be Jewish to love Levy's,' and the copy for the famous Ohrbach's ad, 'I found out about Joan'. Paula Green wrote 'We Try Harder' for Avis. And it was Rita Selden who told Julian Koenig to use 'Lemon' as the headline, instead of 'This Volkswagen Missed the Boat'.

Neither did Bernbach himself endorse an especially macho view of creating advertising. The agency world has always had more than its share of self-glorifying and often rather sad workaholics, such as Claude Hopkins, J. Sterling Getchell (whose death at 41 was partly caused by overwork) and David Ogilvy; Bernbach emphatically wasn't one of them. He went home most days at five o'clock and seldom worked at the weekend. 'You see, David', he once said to Ogilvy, 'I love my family'.

There were many lessons that the industry could and should have learnt from Bernbach, at least during the agency's high-flying years in the fifties and sixties: how to manage an agency culture of psychological safety, collaboration, and relative diversity; that you don't need to be a workaholic to produce great work; the importance of artistry; that it's possible to be assertive without rudeness or aggression; that communicating with your audience is more important than pleasing your clients, or your peers. Sadly, those who claimed Bernbach as an inspiration too often learnt precisely the opposite. They tried to copy the agency's distinctive style, rather than its principles – and mostly did it badly. They interpreted Bill's call to 'do it different' as a license for mere eccentricity. They wanted to emulate his authority with clients, but didn't know how, and instead became merely arrogant and aggressive (or when that failed, resentfully submissive). They wanted to do work that appealed to the advertising village as DDB's did, and they shared Bernbach's rejection of research – but in the process, lost any connection with their real audiences.

There is probably no single explanation as to why the culture of creative departments developed as it did. It was certainly encouraged by role models like DDB alumni Papert Koenig Lois, whose talented but foul-mouthed partners had a reputation for fist fights and throwing things out of windows, and who became an inspiration to CDP and others. In particular, much of the rhetoric of violent rebellion can be traced back to George Lois:

> If you're not a bad boy, if you're not a pain in the ass, you're some mush, in this business. (Frank, p. 80)

And it may be that, as the 'creatives' became superstars, locked in an increasingly high stakes battle for awards and inflated salaries, collaboration and craft skills gave way to a take-no-prisoners culture in which traditional masculine values of individuality and naked aggression made the typical creative department a place few women (and indeed not all men) wanted to be. I've often thought there's an analogy between creative directors in ad agencies and chefs; just because cooking in the home has, in most cultures, been a female preserve, professional cooks have often similarly asserted their masculinity through overwork, bullying and bad language in the workplace – I wonder whether there was a subconscious urge among men who wanted to participate in copywriting's new rock-star status to distance themselves from its traditional association with being a woman's role.

Whatever the reasons, 'creativity' in advertising agencies became identified with an aggressively male, kick-ass, rare-and-bloody fantasy of disruption and revolution. All of which, it seems to me, has not a lot to do with what really matters when it comes to creating popular advertising and famous brands.

But can we get closer to defining what does really matter?

Chapter Fifteen
The Dark Interloper

The word 'creativity' may have been coined in 1927 by the philosopher Alfred North Whitehead, in a difficult book called *Process and Reality*: he seems to have meant by it something like the fundamental principle of freedom and change in all things. From this esoteric and obscure origin, creativity has grown into a popular but ambiguous concept among managers, academics, and the world at large, as well as in the ad business.

So let's begin by looking at the word in these broader contexts.

> Creativity is the ability to produce work that is both novel (i.e. original, unexpected) and appropriate (i.e. useful, adaptive concerning task restraints).

This valiant attempt at a definition is in the opening paragraph of the *Handbook of Creativity*, a weighty summary of academic thinking about the topic edited by Robert Sternberg, Professor of Psychology at Yale. The *Handbook* represents several decades of studying creativity as a branch of psychology, and in their attempts to reclaim the topic from mystics, poets, and the likes of Edward de Bono, academics have done their best to create evidence-based studies about what kind of people are most creative, how creativity can be measured, what conditions most encourage it to flourish, and so on. Such inquiries do all rather hinge on what the word means, though, and the authors acknowledge that there are many possible definitions of the word. However, it seems that this opening definition, or something very like it, has come to achieve quite a high consensus in the field.

So how was this definition arrived at? The first idea behind it is that of originality, or as it was named by Guilford in 1950, 'divergent thinking' – experiments that measure things like 'how many uses can you think of for a brick?' as a test of an individual's 'creativity'. To this, others objected that merely multiplying potentially absurd and irrelevant thoughts shouldn't really count, and that to be truly creative there should also be 'task restraints'; this led to alternative experiments which asked subjects to solve problems, such as pinning a candle to a wall. The resulting consensus definition therefore combines *originality* with *appropriateness*.

This definition has always seemed to me deeply unsatisfactory. Firstly, it seems to leave out a huge territory of what I think of when I think of creativity – it doesn't seem to have anything to say as to why Mozart, or Jackson Pollock, or Ella Fitzgerald (or John Webster) might be thought of as 'creative'. Secondly, it feels to me as if there's a logical contradiction lurking somewhere at the heart of it: if what's needed is something 'appropriate' or 'useful', why is it important to be original, if something *unoriginal* would do the job best? Conversely, if there's some intrinsic value in originality, why try to constrain this with some narrow functional notion of 'appropriateness'?

Nevertheless, this academic definition seems to have become the basis for the standard definitions in the management discourse too. In 2002, the Royal Society for the Encouragement of Arts, Manufactures and Commerce (RSA) published a report called *challenging convention: creativity in organisations*, by Mathilda Joubert. It's clear from the outset that the author of this report identifies 'creativity' with 'innovation', and soon enough this is made explicit:

> …creativity/innovation – terms we use synonymously.

A footnote enlarges on this:

> ...our conception matches the one developed by the National Advisory
> Committee on Creative and Cultural Education: 'imaginative activity fashioned
> so as to produce outcomes that are both original and of value'.

This is obviously similar to the academic definition. But what is the point of
using the word 'creativity' at all if it is *literally* 'synonymous' with innovation? We
get some clues later in the report (which was written for, and based on interviews
with, managers) where we learn more about the relationship between the two
words:

> ... some interviewees reported managers stating that they supported innovation,
> but not creativity...

and this suspicion of 'creativity' was further illuminated by another research
nugget:

> ...some managers... could also believe creative individuals to be disruptive and
> requiring constraint to prevent them from causing major damage.

So we begin to understand that the word 'creativity', while often espoused as
an important quality by managers, may also have a threatening quality about
it. (And ironically, as we saw in the previous chapter, many creative staff in
advertising have done their best to live up to that.) Hence the popularity of
sanitised definitions, which marry the concepts of *originality* and *usefulness/
value*, or the use of 'innovation' as a euphemism for the dangerous word.

But what are these managers so afraid of? Who are these 'disruptive individuals' who
may cause 'major damage' in the organization? To me there's one obvious answer –
they're suspected of being Artists. Wild and crazy guys, rebels, who won't do what
they're told – how can the Organization tolerate and 'manage' such people?

And in fact, that contested boundary leads us right to the heart of the matter.
Because there's a fundamental ambiguity about the derivation of the word
'creative' which is usually unnoticed and unacknowledged – and which, I believe,
applies equally to the noun, 'creativity'. This ambiguity was first explained by the
critic, Raymond Williams, in his valuable book *Keywords*:

> Creative in modern English has a general sense of original and innovating, and
> an associated special sense of productive. It is also used to distinguish certain
> kinds of work, as in **creative writing, the creative arts.** (p.72)

The original English sense of the verb **create** was specifically limited to God's
creation of the world, or at most a King creating a Duke. But

> ...during the C18 each word [**create and creation**] acquired a conscious
> connection with ART. It was in relation to this in C18 that **creative** was
> coined... The decisive development was the conscious and then conventional
> association of **creative** with art and thought... **Creativity**, a general name for
> the faculty, followed in C20. (p.73)

Creativity, Williams says, still carries its inherent connotation of originality and
innovation; yet it has become conventionally attached to the whole area of the
'creative arts', whether or not these are especially original:

> Thus any imitative or stereotyped literary work can be called, by convention,
> **creative writing,** and advertising copywriters officially describe themselves as
> **creative.** (p.74)

Williams, being a Marxist, can't be expected to have had too much time for
copywriters, but his history of the word nails the ambiguity at its heart. We
don't normally distinguish between the sense of creativity as 'making something
original and innovative' and 'making something in the broad field of the creative
arts'. But they are profoundly different.

First of all, this clarifies for me why I found the earlier definitions so unsatisfactory
– for me, 'creativity' is a quality that artists show, and it doesn't necessarily have
that much to do with originality for its own sake. And secondly, it clarifies why
creativity may seem such a dangerous and suspect word in the context of the
organisation– it just sounds too much like Art – and that's why 'innovation' is
often a much safer bet. That might explain why, as we read in a later essay in the
Handbook,

> Creativity in the context of traditional organizational theories has been seen as

a *dark interloper of irrationality and a disruptive force* that destabilizes the security of rule-bound thinking. (p.377, *emphasis added*).

And thirdly, this helps explain why the preferred definitions of creativity in academia and in management emphasise *innovation* and *usefulness*, while sidelining any suggestion of aesthetics. This kind of definition leaves plenty of space for new inventions and clever ideas, but it reduces creativity to something essentially functional.

The great Bob Hoffman recently came to the same conclusion, but he expressed it more pithily:

> Sure, the guy who printed the tickets to *Hamlet*, or made the popcorn, or counted the proceeds, may have found creative ways to do so. But he didn't write the fucking play.

The kind of creativity that matters in the context of advertising and of brands is not functional innovation. It is not even *originality* per se; you will recall from an earlier chapter how this plays only a modest part in the creation of artefacts that achieve popularity or fame. (I first argued these points as long ago as 2010 in a TEDx talk which is perhaps still worth viewing.) No, what we really need to be looking for when we use the word creativity in our business is *artistry*. This is the 'dark interloper of rationality', what Bill Bernbach called 'the intangible thing that business so mistrusts' – but which effective advertising is also so dependent on.

And artistry is not just about coming up with abstract ideas, but involves creating actual, embodied works. As Bob Hoffman would put it, you've got to write the fucking play – and then, indeed, you have to cast it and act it and build the sets and play the music and design the lighting and so on, because it's every word and gesture and nuance and detail of the actual performance that adds up to whether the audience applaud and come back next week, or just throw orange peels at you. This is what we need to remember when we think about creativity, and it's so important I shall make it the theme of my next chapter.

Chapter Sixteen
The Trouble With Ideas

When we talk about creativity in advertising, we should principally mean one thing only –the creation of tangible, specific, *embodied* works that only confront the public as finished wholes. These are not abstractions. If we say we 'have ideas' or 'devise strategies' these are only, at best, part of the means to the end of creating an actual work, an actual show. We are not in the business of ideas.

I know some people will find this statement heretical, or even baffling, because the use of the word 'idea' to describe the outcome of the creative process in advertising is so universal, and has a long history. The great James Webb Young titled his best selling short book *A Technique for Producing Ideas*. In any advertising interview, presentation or *Campaign* article it is a safe bet that you will find phrases like these:

How advertising's big *ideas* are born [feature headline]

Why all agencies need to look for the big *idea* [column headline]

.X, Head of Marketing at Debenhams, says what retailers need right now from agencies is 'great creative *ideas* that differentiate our message from those of competitors'…

.Y, Chairman of the Jury and ECD said the judges looked for the 'biggest and freshest *ideas*'

The common variant, 'big idea', can be attributed to David Ogilvy. The last time I was inside O&M in London the quote was all over one wall:

Unless your advertising contains a big idea, it will pass like a ship in the night.

This is well known. Yet not so many people seem to have read it in its original context, *Ogilvy on Advertising*, where the author admits that

I doubt if more than one campaign in a hundred contains a big idea. I am supposed to be one of the more fertile inventors of big ideas, but in my long career as a copywriter I have not had more than twenty (p.16).

But what did Ogilvy mean by a big idea? He goes on to give a few examples:

+ the Pepperidge Farm horse drawn van (an image which came to Ogilvy in a dream)

+ the Merrill Lynch bulls

+ the Hathaway eye patch

+ the slogan 'Dove doesn't dry your skin the way soap can'

+ The American Express commercial format, 'Do You Know Me?'

+ The Marlboro Cowboy.

It's clear that in every case what Ogilvy means by a 'big idea' is not an abstraction, but something specific and tangible: a visual image, a line, or a commercial format. In fact, these are all good examples of successful and long-lived *distinctive assets* or *fluent devices*, which we discussed in an earlier chapter.

(I think it likely that when Rosser Reeves stressed the importance of the USP, what was really working in his ads were tangible distinctive assets, all built by endless repetition: visual images such as the Anacin head with hammers, or slogans: 'Wonderbread Helps Build Strong Bodies 8 Ways', or 'M&Ms melt in your mouth, not in your hand'. The power lay in specific and memorable images or strings of words, not in abstract ideas.)

The problem is that, for most people today, the word 'idea' does not mean what Ogilvy intended by it. It *may* usefully mean that early stage in the creative process when something is glimpsed but yet unformed: as when John Webster would quietly mention, 'I've had an idea' and we'd all go off to his office, or in the title of Bill Backer's memoir, *The Care and Feeding of Ideas*. In this sense, an idea is a starting point, but it is very far from being the finished article.

This amount of weight I think the word can take, but *idea* is also used as if it meant many other things; and it is often unclear in casual advertising discourse what exactly it does mean. This can be part of the word's usefulness, because you don't have to specify whether you're talking about an ad, an end-line, a strategy, a moment of inspiration, a campaign theme, or a distinctive asset. But these are all different things, and it would be better to give them different names.

However, the word is at its most dangerous when, as it frequently does, it means something else again – the 'creative idea' that is imagined as some Platonic abstraction behind the ad or campaign, which can be defined in words and written down in a strategy document, and from which all the mere 'executions' can be generated in a way that will ensure consistency and control. It is very analogous to the notion of 'brand essence' in this respect. But it is, if anything, even less meaningful.

Try for a moment this experiment. Think of an ad or a campaign that you admire (preferably one that you also believe to be effective). Now write down what you think is the 'creative idea' behind it.

I have tried this many times with groups of people who speak casually about creative ideas and I can promise you two things. However plausible your form of words is, it is only one of an infinite number of plausible answers. What's more, if you gave any of these 'ideas', or even all of them, to someone who had never seen the actual ad, they would have no conceivable way of reconstructing the ad itself.

To make the point even simpler, try to formulate the 'creative idea' behind:

- *The Sopranos*
- *Toy Story*
- 'Rock Around the Clock'
- Edward Hopper's 'Nighthawks'
- *Peanuts*
- Mozart's 40th Symphony

Or indeed anything else. At best, you will have come up a banal and generic summary of the content, or, if you're cleverer, some interpretation of what you think its 'themes' are about. In neither case will you be within a million miles of even the simplest actual work.

The fundamental, philosophical errors behind this illusion are not just that the 'meaning' of a work can be separated from the work itself, but that the meaning, once separated, is somehow more important than the thing itself. It's a dangerous habit which is also common in literary criticism, as Susan Sontag pointed out in her brilliant essay 'Against Interpretation':

> The modern style of interpretation excavates, and, as it excavates, destroys; it digs behind the text to find a sub-text which is the true one.

Critical readers like to do this, for the same reason that managers like to reduce ads to 'creative ideas', and brands to 'essences' – it appears to make the implicit work of art, in all its complexity, into something explicit, definable, controlled.

> …one tames the work of art. Interpretation makes art manageable, conformable.

It's a way of fitting those crazy artists safely into the organization, again.

The profound danger of this philosophical error was brought home to me many years ago when I was working on a global brand for a packaged goods client who prided themselves on their marketing sophistication . After much work, we had come up with an end line or slogan for the brand which seemed to us to suggest endless possibilities for commercials, and which matched at a deep level the lengthy 'brand essence' work we had already done. The client totally agreed, and seemed equally excited. We were all keen to move forward to what would have really mattered – making some actual ads – when the marketing director said, 'Of course, we'll have to know what the creative idea is first'.

We looked blankly. Unconsciously channelling David Ogilvy, I said, 'That line *is* the creative idea'. The clients looked at me pityingly. 'No, that's just a line. We need to know what the idea is behind it before we can approve any further work.'

I need not tell you that we spent the next eighteen months in sterile arguments about the answer to this unanswerable question until we had all lost any enthusiasm for the campaign (and almost lost the will to live). Not only did they want to 'dig behind the text' to find a 'sub-text which is the true one'; they wanted to do this for a text that hadn't even been written yet.

In 2007, Cadbury produced a striking commercial which attracted much public attention – it showed a man in a gorilla suit sitting at the drums, playing loudly and angrily along to the Phil Collins song, 'In the Air Tonight'. It was the early days of YouTube, and many people were sharing it online and arguing about what it meant and why they found it so compelling. History is not clear as to whether this ad sold a lot of chocolate or not – there are conflicting accounts that do the rounds – though I am inclined to think that, as the ad was famous, popular (voted the nation's favourite ad) , and clearly identified with the Cadbury brand through a subtle use of colour as a distinctive asset, it very probably did. The interesting thing, though, is what Cadbury did next.

The marketing director, Phil Rumbol, had obviously gone to hell and back to sell this mystifying ad to the Cadbury management. Somewhere along the way, he had succeeded in persuading them (and perhaps himself) that what they were buying was not a drumming gorilla, but a creative idea, and that idea was 'joy'. Never mind that this word is far from an obvious interpretation of the ambiguous image we see and hear (the Collins song is a very bitter one about his marriage breakup).

So to follow the ad's popular success, the next commercial featured neither gorilla, nor drums, nor anything like them. Instead it showed a lot of trucks driving around very fast. In the clients' minds, this presumably represented a continuation of the creative idea. But it didn't in anyone else's, and the new ad flopped totally. The trucks commercial simply lacked all the odd, distinctive, and engaging qualities of that actual gorilla banging those actual drums .

My guess is that the client organisation, and perhaps the agency too, had come to believe so powerfully in this spurious 'creative idea' that they no longer saw what was in front of them – the gorilla had become a mere disposable 'execution', while 'joy' could be represented at will by just about anything else. Except that, of course, it couldn't. That original film, which the author and director Juan Cabral had gone to extreme lengths to create in a very precise way, was both emotionally engaging to the public, and a great example of Byron Sharp's 'meaningless distinctive'. It raised mental availability of Cadbury's and created what could have become a valuable distinctive asset (even today I bet most people can name the brand correctly when they see that gorilla). But in their typical rush to abstraction, the client threw all this away.

Susan Sontag's essay ends with a plea to *see* again, to value and experience what's actually in front of us, not to focus just on whatever ideas or interpretations we choose to read into it:

> What is important now is to recover our senses. We must learn to see more, to hear more, to feel more…The function of criticism should be to show *how it is what it is*, even *that it is what it is*, rather than to show what it means.

When we study ads, let us look at what is there in front of us, not at some abstract idea in our heads. Throughout this book, I have tried to show that the power of any advertisement (or brand, or celebrity) lies not in some imagined, unique idea or essence, but in the complete, embodied detail of what the audience experience with their senses. The Barclaycard films, 'Hilltop', Sunny Jim with his stick and pigtail, the Honey Monster with his deep voice and babyish antics, the drumming gorilla, all make their effects on their audiences and lodge in their memories and influence their behaviours because of the specific realities of what they look like, how they sound and behave, how their stories or melodies elapse in time – not because of any single meaning that we might attach to them, let alone some Platonic 'idea' supposed to precede or shape them. 'Aesthetics' may be what David Ogilvy would have called a high-falutin word, but its basic meaning is from Greek *aisthesis*, perception through the senses – that is why we use it to generalise about the visual arts, music, or anything else that we can only fully appreciate at first at a sensual level. Advertising is very rarely the same thing as 'high art', but it has this in common with it.

People do of course read meanings into things, and that is part of the pleasure and fascination they find in them. They may interpret 'Hilltop' as a response to the Vietnam War, or David Beckham's haircut as an act of penitence or fatherhood. But there is never a single 'correct' interpretation, and the richness of a work is often indicated by the range and diversity of interpretations it can evoke – that is why the plays of Shakespeare or the symphonies of Beethoven continue to fascinate and reward. The work, the performance itself comes first, in its embodied form, and the multiplicity of meanings are what we read into it.

Interpretations are our left brain hemisphere's attempt to reduce the complexity of what we perceive to something simple and definable. It is a natural part of our response, and part of our pleasure. But as with art, the full sense we make of any aesthetic artefact is only possible with the active involvement of the right brain, which has the capacity to see the whole, to integrate and make sense of without analysing, and which connects directly with our emotions in a way that the analytical left brain never can. As Orlando Wood explains it:

> …the right hemisphere is undoubtedly more important for creativity; it sees the whole and is much better able to make connections between seemingly unrelated things. It plays with language and mixes words up in interesting and unexpected ways, can see things on different levels, see parallels, understand metaphor and is what helps us to distinguish humour from lies. It likes to see new in the familiar – relationships between things – rather than shock with the novel. It's interested in the living, is the mediator of empathic identification and is pre-eminent in its ability to understand meaning and feeling through inflection of the voice, and gestures of the face and body.

Not only are these things important when creating work, but they are also the features of advertising that *attract and sustain attention in audiences* (the right hemisphere is responsible for the apprehension of anything new at the 'edges of our awareness'), that *elicit an emotional response* (the right hemisphere is responsible for unconscious emotional processing and is dominant in all forms of emotional perception and expression), and that *make things memorable* (emotions are responsible for imprinting memory, and the right hemisphere is dominant in autobiographical memory). So this seems pretty close to me to what is important when we use the term 'creativity' in advertising – and what we should be aiming for.

In Iain McGilchrist's words, the right brain hemisphere experiences the world as 'unique, embodied, and implicit' and these are also the characteristics of what we actually produce when we make commercials, print ads, posters, films, animations, pack designs, logos, characters, copy. *Unique*, because nothing is exactly like any of them but itself; *embodied*, because they exist only in what is perceived through the senses; *implicit*, because the meanings we read into them are not inherent or fixed, but endlessly negotiable.

Creativity in advertising, then, must mean the task of creating such actual, embodied works and performances, that impact on the audience's right brain hemisphere. We should not make the mistake, as Cadbury did, of focusing only on some general, abstract and explicit 'creative idea', while losing sight of the unique, embodied and implicit drumming gorilla right in front of us.

Conclusion

Reclaiming Creativity

Perhaps we should just stop using the word *creativity* altogether. The world, and even the advertising profession, got along without it very well for a long time – it was a word unknown to Barnum, or Claude Hopkins, or Minnie Maud Hanff – and I think I got along without it quite well enough in the first twelve chapters of this book.

Because it seems to me that in the advertising world today, the way the word is used is a big part of the problem we're facing. It has come to signify, not entertainment and artistry and popular appeal, but an esoteric and self-validating cult that refuses to define or discuss itself. It appears to despise wit, playfulness, and fun, and stands instead for negative values of aggression and destruction. It takes itself terribly seriously, is terrified of appearing too popular, and in the name of perpetual revolution rejects everything that made past advertising appealing and historic brands successful. If that's all the word *creativity* is ever going to mean, we would be better off without it.

But realistically, I fear this genie is now out of its bottle, and the word is not going to go away. In which case, I think we in the advertising business need to make it clear what we really do want it to mean in the context of our business. Perhaps it is not too late to reclaim it from the unhelpful connotations it has acquired in the last half century or so.

So here is my manifesto for reclaiming 'creativity':

- First, we need to stop any pretence that creativity is simply beyond discussion.

- We need to stop lazily equating it to some crude 'shock and awe' notion of originality for its own sake.

- We need to stop using the word as a battle cry in agency turf wars, and to end the self-referencing and sterile circularity of defining it as 'whatever wins awards'.

- We should recognise that creativity is to do with crafting actual advertisements, or other embodied performances – not just about having bright ideas or devising strategies. These are not unimportant, but they are only means to an end.

- I see no point in using the word creativity as a synonym for *innovation*, which is a perfectly good word in its own right.

- Above all, we need to stop behaving as if creativity in advertising could ever be considered without any reference to the public that we are in business to address, to woo, and to entertain. Creativity is the artistry and imagination we need in order to achieve popularity and fame for the brands we advertise.

Not all advertising has to be entertaining. There is an important place for information and argument in advertising too. But I have tried to show throughout this book that advertising as entertainment stands in a long, honourable (if not always respectable) tradition of singing pedlars, mountebanks, and medicine shows, which used their performances not just to attract the crowds, but to win their custom, and to get them coming back for more. The growth of the mass media, and their value to advertisers, followed directly from this tradition. And from their outset in the nineteenth century, brands routinely used all these techniques and platforms to build and maintain their fame, popularity, and distinctiveness.

What Howard Gossage wrote in the sixties is even more important today, in an era when highly targeted and interruptive advertising is having the principal effect of irritating and alienating its audience:

> The buying of time and space is not the taking out of a hunting license on someone's private preserve, but the renting of a stage on which we may perform.

Whatever kind of stage we use, we must never forget that we are putting on a show, and our sole intent is to have a favourable effect on the audience. If creativity is to mean anything useful, it is the art and skill of winning and keeping that audience. ·

Our ability to please the public matters, not just because history shows this is generally the best way to build lasting brands, but because advertising's license to have a hearing at all ultimately depends on its ability to engage the public, not to insult it. To quote Bob Hoffman again:

> If we want there to be an audience for advertising, if we want people to engage with what we do, we have to do a lot better. We have to make advertising beautiful, and interesting, and entertaining.

There is no reason we can't apply the word creativity firmly to this kind of production. For an example of what this might look like, read Ed Catmull's *Creativity, Inc.*, the fascinating story of how Pixar was built up. What Catmull has to say about creativity is worth hearing, because Pixar films are a brilliant example of embodied work that is richly detailed, beautifully crafted, and above all, popular. After all, people pay good money to see Pixar films – while, at the moment, they'll pay to avoid seeing advertising.

We learn from Catmull's book that making a Pixar film is far from being a momentary revelation of a 'big idea' (though many moments of epiphany may occur along the way) – it's a persistent, iterative process of trying things out, improving them, arguing about them, resolving those arguments, re-drawing, re-writing, re-shooting, editing, until gradually the finished product emerges in all its detail. To do this requires the ability to give and receive candid feedback, to tolerate mess, uncertainty and conflict, to live with the chance of failure, and to understand that the overall shape of the end product may not become clear until late in its development. As one of its principal writers remarked of the Pixar film, *Up*:

> It wasn't a matter of unearthing a buried story; in the beginning, there was no story.

It's from the interactions between the many people involved in creating a film that new and eventually better things continually emerge – not just a host of details, but the overall flow and emotional structure of the piece. Pixar films are 'unique, embodied, and implicit', and their creation, like their appreciation, depends on the active involvement of the right brain hemisphere. Yet this doesn't mean any of it can't be talked about. Indeed, despite the difficulties of putting things into words, and the sensitivities of interpersonal relationships, it all *has* to be talked about. The picture that emerges of the Pixar culture is by no means without stress or conflict, but it is distinctly not a world of people flouncing out of rooms, refusing to change things, or throwing typewriters out of windows. It is a place where people may continually fail to be perfect, yet they work through it and get things done.

I think much the same would be true of the cases I have reviewed at length in this book. We are lucky enough to have detailed accounts of how 'Hilltop' was created, and also Honey Monster. In both cases, the finished product emerges from a complex series of interactions and negotiations between a wide range of people. They are not 'light-bulb' moments, or simple inspirations from on high.

The Honey Monster story is typical of how John Webster worked. He was interested in research because, like Pixar, he wanted his work above all to be popular. If real people didn't enjoy what he'd written, or if it rubbed them up the wrong way, he'd try and find a way to recast the ad so that it worked. He was always curious, always experimenting, and talking about the work was for him not a threat, but always an opportunity. When stuck, he would go and talk to whoever happened to be around (after hours, that was often the security guard) and that conversation would give him the opening he needed to go on.

The creation of the Barclaycard films, as I recall it, emerged in a similar way from continual exchanges between Atkinson, Lloyd, and the agency writers and producers, and included endless rewrites and adjustments throughout the often eventful location shoots. Stories like these, which I think are not uncommon, remind us that creativity is not some magical or ineffable property which mysteriously appears of its own accord. It is the outcome of talented people finding ways to work together, with a common goal, until the wonderful thing finally emerges.

There is no simple formula for how this happens. One crucial thing is that the people involved are prepared to stick with it and work through the anxieties of the creative process. This need not be all sweetness and light, as organisational guru Ralph Stacey explains in this dense but profound paragraph:

> The capacity for emergent new ways of talking is fundamental to organisational creativity... The dynamics of more fluid, spontaneous conversation rely on enough trust and ability to live with anxiety, as well as power relations that are both co-operative and competitive at the same time and rhetorical conversational practices that do not block exploration.

Skills for 'keeping the conversation open' in this way can be learnt and encouraged, as they are at Pixar: being able to listen, to remain open-minded, to accept feedback, to tolerate frustration – equally, to stand up for what you feel passionate about, to say uncomfortable things, to ask difficult questions. But the process can also be, and generally benefits from being, fun. The creative process flourishes best in an environment of psychological safety, in which people feel free to play around, make silly suggestions, and be open and unguarded with each other. Evenings in the pub and long lunches may not be the only way of doing this, but they used to help, and should not be entirely despised.

It would be rash to sound too prescriptive about what constitutes a culture of creativity. But I suspect it is important to have a common goal. The people working together must share enough common ground about their purpose, and the kind of thing they are trying to create. Advertising today too often lacks that common goal. Some are trying to win awards, some are trying to please their bosses, some are trying to produce work that can be logically justified, some are trying to look fashionable, some don't want to do it at all. If only they could all agree that their task is to produce advertising that is popular, distinctive, and famous!

*

And yet, and yet... I realise, as I try to draw to a close, that it's also all too easy for our idea of creativity to become, as Ogilvy would have said, too high-falutin. We can't afford to let 'creativity' give itself too many airs and graces – I'm sure this has been part of its problem – so if we are to go on using the word we need to guard against that. We are not creating a work of high art – we are putting on a show. And creativity doesn't have to be complicated. As well as in the elaborate, highly skilled performance, it may just as well be found in the innocent, spontaneous gesture – the doodling of a face on a bowl of soup, the naming of a brand after a bistro you walked past, the improvised mini-dress made from a Union Jack.

As correctives, let's make regular visits to the Museum of Brands, and look at the Joe 90 Bubble Bath and the Spice Girls potato crisps. Let's read Mark Borkowski's outrageous history of the stuntsmen, fixers, and fakers who created the Hollywood celebrity industry, *The Fame Formula*. Let's read celebrity memoirs, and the candid histories of brands, and remind ourselves of the complex series of events, gestures, and responses that actually create fame. And when we are tempted to take what we do too seriously, let's paraphrase Michael Winner : 'Calm down dear, it's only an advert!'.

And let's never forget Barnum's great ironical word for what he did, Humbug. Creativity is to be found in the FeeJee Mermaid as much as in the arias of Jenny Lind. It exists in the gestures of buying Jumbo the elephant, or promising a five cent Coke to every US serviceman around the world, as well as in the lovingly crafted poster or TV commercial. Creativity must include the improvisatory and the responsive, the embracing of a silly nickname or an unexpected turn of events, a haircut, or a whim to wear a sarong. Advertising may be a serious business, but the creativity it needs mustn't always take itself too seriously. 'Goodness gracious!' said Minnie Maud Hanff – 'a breakfast cereal isn't all life, is it?'. She wrote the first Force ads in a New York streetcar, while *Toy Story* took years to make – yet it remains to be seen whether Buzz Lightyear will be as well remembered after a century as Sunny Jim.

I'm reminded of another passage from Claude Bonnange and Chantal Thomas, words which partly inspired me to write this book:

> *Tout se passe comme si le métier de publicitaire, qui avait commencé dans une atmosphère de spontaneité et d'invention artisanale, sur un fond de gratuité amusée, s'était, en passant à une phase industrielle, soumis à des injonctions de prévision et d'organisation qui, en lui donnant une place assignée dans un processus de rentabilité, le privaient de tout élan ludique, de sa fraîcheur originelle (p.25).*

> It's as if the craft of advertising, which had started in an atmosphere of spontaneity and homespun invention, founded in fun and frivolity, has passed into its industrial phase, where it is subject to prescriptive organisational rules. While these rules justify its place in the grand scheme of business, they have stripped it of all its playful exuberance and its original energy (author's translation).

Bonnange and Thomas were lamenting, and quite rightly, the way that advertising's willingness to submit to managerial culture had stifled its spontaneity and invention. But, ironically, I fear that today's concept of 'creativity' has had just as bad an effect. We need to rediscover a kind of creativity that includes and celebrates exuberance, fun and frivolity – and a healthy dose of humbug. Creativity that is a process of imagination and artistry, producing campaigns that are popular, enjoyable, and famous. A creativity that is not in any way opposed to effectiveness in advertising, but is in reality its most powerful engine.

Notes

These limited notes are meant to give specific references which wouldn't otherwise be clear from the text, some indications of further reading on specific topics I've skated over, and in a few cases to add some more information. References to the Bibliography are all given by author's name, with date where needed.

Preface

ix   von Mises: quoted in Driver and Foxall 1984, p.62.

x   'Sometimes the ads are better than the programmes': source TGI, an annual survey now owned by Kantar Media.

     Jeff Bezos: interviewed in 1997 by Jeffrey Seglin. https://www.inc.com/magazine/19970901/1314 viewed on 3/9/20.

xi   'The most important search engine remains the one in your head': I'm sure I heard this line at a conference or somewhere, but I have no recollection who I got it from. I repeat it, though I don't think I invented it, because it's so true and so well-expressed. (I explored the thought further, with an example, in Feldwick 2019.)

Chapter 1: Richard Latham's Rug

6   Barclaycard IPA case: the 'official' story is in Feldwick 1997.

11   For the full story of Ernest Dichter and other quasi-Freudian researchers, see Samuel; also, Feldwick 2015, Chapters 5 and 6.

12   '...most of what goes on in our minds is unconscious': e.g. Wilson, Kahneman.

17   Orlando Wood quote: from publicity material for System1. It seems to me the most elegant summary, so I'm glad to have preserved it.

18   'Torches of Freedom': Ewen, pp.3-4.

Chapter 2: From Salesmanship to Showmanship

24   'An earlier version of this story' : referring to Feldwick 2005. Quote from Bullmore 2008.

25   Containing, avoiding, or working through anxiety: my ideas on the anxiety in organisations caused by creative processes, and the various 'flight or fight' responses to it, referred to throughout this book, have been shaped by a number of writers including Menzies, Hirschhorn, de Board, Argyris and Schön, and Stacey. Catmull's book is also relevant. The topic was central to the dissertation I submitted for my Master's in Organisational Consulting (Feldwick 2012).

Chapter 3: Who Framed Sunny Jim?

32   Sunny Jim story: Source, Margerum, with all references. unless otherwise. Lears and Rutherford each deal at length with the self-image of the advertising business.

35   'the price of a loaf of bread': https://fraser.stlouisfed.org/title/bulletin-united-states-bureau-labor-3943/july-1905-477618/retail-prices-food-498513?start_page=179 viewed on 29/09/20

41   Vic Norman's trip to LA: the uneasy relationship between Madison Avenue and Hollywood has persisted into the twenty-first century. Scott

Donaton's *Madison and Vine* (2004) made an eloquent argument for the two industries to work more closely together in an era when the traditional business model of each was under severe threat. As a movement, this was sidelined almost immediately, as advertisers and agencies became mesmerised instead by social media, ad-tech, and 'brand purpose'. But entrepreneurs quietly continue to find opportunities for mutual benefit, as they have always done: as I write, the latest James Bond Omega watch – tied in with a film that hasn't even been released yet – is selling fast at over $50,000 a piece, and the Omega share price has doubled in the past few months on the back of it.

42   'Don't treat your subject lightly...': Hopkins 1923/1986, p.261

'Don't *sing* your selling message...': Ogilvy 1963/2013, p.148

'Merely to let your imagination run riot...': As his former head of PR explains (Doris Willens, Chapter 12) Bernbach had a basic 'stump speech' which he endlessly repeated with variations throughout his career. He kept the material for this on index cards, and after his death Willens extracted the most-used quotes for a small volume published by DDB called *Bill Bernbach Said*; unless specified otherwise, this is my source for all Bernbach quotes.

Chapter 4: Because singers sell soap, Mr Norman

Principal sources for the history of mountebanks and medicine shows: McNamara, Anderson.

45   'We want above all...': Bonnange and Thomas, p.23. *'Nous voulons surtout, à travers ce bref survol historique, pointer un aspect de la publicité actuellement trop oublié : une certain candeur, une naïveté du phénomène publicitaire à ses débuts. Il part tout autant d'une envie de vendre que d'un goût du spectacle, de la parade verbale, du jeu théatral. Les deux sont intimement liés: le fait de vendre n'étant qu'un élément dans la mise en œuvre d'une scène de la communication dont la richesse dépasse de beaucoup le rapport duel vendeur/acheteur... et les gens achèteront non en raison d'un besoin (même illusoire), mais comme acte de participation, adhésion amusée au divertissement d'un moment crée par le camelot de la rue.'*

48   'The arrival of a circus in the village...': ibid., p.23. *'Ou bien a l'arriveé*

d'un cirque dans un village, aux dandinements des éléphants, aux cabrioles des écuyères, aux pitreries des clowns dans la rue centrale: c'étaient les préliminaires du <<vrai>> spectacle, une publicité pour attirer le public. Mais c'était déja, avant la séance du soir, une manifestation du cirque dans la ville.'

'The buying of time, or space...': p. 20 in 'Is There Any Hope For Advertising?' in Gossage.

49   Thomas Coryat quotes: McNamara, p.5.

Chapter 5: From Barnum to Brands

59   Principal sources for Barnum throughout: Saxon, Adams, Cook.

63   Source for Quaker Oats history and quotes: Marquette.

71   'Advertising textbooks': e.g. Aaker, Batra and Myers 1992, Rossiter and Percy 1987, Wells, Burnett and Moriarty 1992, Hardy, Powell and McCrury 2019. (Though Ambler and Teller 2007 contains one index reference to 'fame of a brand' – in a chapter by Peter Field. *Exceptio probat regulum.*)

73   'Sociologists would argue': e.g. Fiske, or Jenkins.

Chapter 6: David Beckham's Sarong

87   'the histories of the great brands': a sweeping generalisation, I know. But the following chapter could equally have been written about, say, Nike, or Apple, as a reading of Knight or Isaacson will show.

Chapter 7: Energy, Essence and Icons

89   'This kind of research': in my 2002 book *What Is Brand Equity, Anyway?*, I dealt with the contradictory meanings and measurements of 'brand equity' at greater length than the subject probably ever deserved.

90   Brand Foundations structure: some of the language, it must be admitted, sounded better in French. 'The fight' was '*le combat*', and '*le client imaginaire*' sounded like a lost play by Molière.

Chapter 8: A Face in the Piazza Navona

111 P.G. Tips case history: Cooper et al. This, Barclaycard, and all IPA case histories are available to subscribers at www.warc.com . There is also a good IPA video about the history of P.G.Tips advertising at https://www.thinkbox.tv/case-studies/brand-films/pg-tips/ viewed on 29/09/20.

112 Single Source data: the best summary, with full references, is in Broadbent, Part Two. See also Jones 1995.

113 'Equilibrium Share Of Voice': Jones 1992, pp. 89-97; Binet and Field 2007, pp. 41-49.

Chapter 9: Broadcast to Go Big

126 Piano Staircase: the film can be found here: https://www.youtube.com/watch?v=SByymar3bds (viewed on 03/09/20). This short video won the Cyber Grand Prix at Cannes in 2009. What the film does not make clear is that the installation was in place for one day only, so its actual social impact was trivial. It is described as an experiment, but no details are given beyond the single figure of a 66% increase in people using the stairs, and I have been unable to find that it was ever written up or published. As what used to be unfashionably known as a 'publicity stunt' – an event designed to get coverage in the media – the video certainly achieved a degree of fame, though probably more among other communication professionals than with the general public. Its real skill was to tick all the fashionable boxes required to win a creative award in 2009: apparently 'viral' (though not in reality, as I've argued), using digital social media, 'experiential', with an ostensible 'social purpose', demonstrating 'innovation' and 'disruption' – and not looking like 'an advert'. The stunt was harmless enough in itself, but its canonisation as a model for what agencies should all be aspiring to produce contributed to the deplorable trend which I describe in Part Four of this book. And creative awards have become more and more obsessed with 'social purpose' rather than commercial success, a worrying phenomenon that has been brilliantly eviscerated by Steve Harrison in *Can't Sell, Won't Sell*.

Chapter 11: Give the Lion Wings

140 Venice: mostly from John Julius Norwich.

142 Dulux: personal experience.

   Andrex: anecdotal, but confirmed by Andrex website https://www.andrex.co.uk/history-of-andrex viewed on 3/9/20.

143 P.G Tips Chimps: Fletcher, p.201. The original agency was Spottiswoode, which merged with Davidson Pearce Berry and Tuck in 1970. Perhaps the finest years of the Chimps campaign were the early seventies, under the creative leadership of Norman Berry. Davidson Pearce Berry and Spottiswoode was bought by BMP in 1988 where John Webster revived the campaign in the 1990s. The last Chimps ad ran in 2002.

   'Why a Polar Bear?': Carter, p.25.

144 'Just Like That' : Tommy Cooper, in case you didn't know.

146 Nike Swoosh: Knight, pp. 180-181. Twelve years later, Knight also gave Davidson 500 Nike shares, today worth millions.

   Pudsey Bear: https://www.bbc.co.uk/news/uk-england-leeds-30024318 viewed on 3/9/20.

147 Bailey's: Gluckman, p. 28.

   Apple: Isaacson, p. 58 .

   Meerkats: personal communication.

148 Knorrli: *Ein Tag Mit Knorrli* is well worth watching and can now be found on the Knorr Schweiz YouTube channel. https://www.youtube.com/watch?v=2koGySt4Kn0 viewed on 03/09/20.

149 Centraal Beheer: campaign described in Feldwick 2015, pp. 147-8. Most commercials easily found on YouTube.

   Granola Bars: Quaker Harvest Crunch. The squirrels commercial can be seen here: https://www.youtube.com/watch?v=O05BaAnGEQc viewed on 03/09/20

Chapter 12: Infinitely Multiply

Much of what I describe in this chapter has been rediscovered in the twenty-first century under names like 'fandom studies', and scholars like Henry Jenkins have published fascinating analyses of how contemporary audiences participate in the creation of fame. But while the media in which they can do this are new, I want to stress that the basic principles of public participation in the creation of fame go back to Barnum and beyond.

153 Social Media in the Roman Empire: Standage.

154 Epidemiology: ironically, this chapter was written during the first 'lockdown' stage of the COVID19 pandemic in 2020. I was helped a lot understanding the subject by Kucharski's timely book, though sadly the theory didn't do so much to contain the spread of the disease in the UK.

158 'Bubbles' and 'The New Frock': McQueen, pp. 46-50

Chapter 13: The C Word

As well as Frank, Delaney, Fletcher, Fox and Cracknell have been valuable sources for the history of UK and US ad agencies; Mayer gives a contemporary account of agencies including DDB and Ogilvy in the fifties.

172 DDB 'developed a reputation for refusing to do clients' bidding': though according to Willens it was Ned Doyle, ex-US Marine and ten years Bernbach's senior, who was prepared to fire clients, while Bernbach himself lived in terror of losing agency income. Despite the agency's 'take-it-or-leave-it' rhetoric, Bernbach's real skills lay in charming clients to accept work, and in persuading his creative teams to write 'something even better' when a client was misguided enough to turn it down.

Ogilvy on Creativity: in Ogilvy 1983, p. 24.

'deliberately eschewing many of the techniques': it's clear from many references in Willens that slogans, jingles, characters, etc. were actually anathema to Bernbach's successors. In time, this ban would extend to any kind of campaignable property: 'The agency's free-wheeling creatives didn't especially relish campaign work in any case. They preferred doing one-off ads, one at a time, custom made.' Willens quotes Barry Loughrane, CEO in the years after Bernbach's death: 'We could go into an art directors show and win 50 awards. But nobody would ever see that advertising. Totally invisible. People remember campaigns, and we weren't doing campaigns.' (pp.166,167). The dominance of DDB by such a cult of creativity was a major factor in the agency's decline through the 70s and 80s, and set a pattern which too many other agencies subsequently copied (including the one I worked for).

173   Rosser Reeves at AWANY: Frank, p. 92.

174   Cannes and Venice in the 70s: Fletcher, p.129.

Jeremy Bullmore quotes: 1978 speech at the inaugural meeting of the Account Planning Group in London, Bullmore 1991, p.167; Fletcher, p.130.

175   Gold TV Awards in 1976: I am grateful to the History of Advertising Trust for finding this information in contemporary copies of *Campaign*.

Chapter 14: Blowing Shit Up

180   John Hegarty: quoted in Cracknell, p.7.

181   Ads written by women: mostly from Fox, but the story about Rita Selden and 'Lemon' is in Imseng, p.46, and the Ohrbach's ad is credited in Willens, who also has interesting material about Bernbach's propensity to take total credit for ads when he had only written the headline. Despite the importance of their contributions, women in DDB were still paid less and discriminated against in other ways, as was typical of the time.

Bernbach, 'I love my family': quoted, to his credit, by Ogilvy himself (1983, p. 205).

Psychological safety: for a definition and evidence see Edmondson.

Chapter 15: The Dark Interloper

184   Guilford: Sternberg, pp.252-3

187   Bob Hoffman : 2016 speech at the IAPA/ADFX Awards in Dublin. Hoffman 2018.

Chapter 16: The Trouble With Ideas

189   Ogilvy on Big Ideas: Ogilvy 1983. pp.16ff.

192   Gorilla ad: an important article including interviews with Rumbol and Cabral is at https://www.theguardian.com/media-network/2016/jan/07/how-we-made-cadburys-gorilla-ad viewed on 03/09/20

194   Orlando Wood: personal communication.

Conclusion

200   Stacey quote: Stacey 2011, p.346. My thinking about the emergent nature of both creative processes and of brands has been much influenced by Stacey's work. By 'emergent' I do not mean they just mysteriously happen, as if without human agency. As Stacey argues in several places, the idea of 'emergence' is never incompatible with human intention: 'intention and emergence are not polarised' (Stacey 2011, p.309). What emerges, emerges from our various intentions, as they interact. Emergence never implies passivity, just an acceptance that you can never control what happens next.

201   Michael Winner: in a long-running TV campaign launched in 2003 for insurance brand, Esure, film director and celebrity Winner popularised the catchphrase 'Calm down, dear, it's a commercial!'. The original commercial can be viewed at https://www.youtube.com/watch?v=efl5pFTFnBU, viewed on 03/09/20. Some criticised this at the time as sexist condescension, even before David Cameron infuriated many by using the phrase 'Calm down, dear!' to Angela Eagle in a Commons debate in 2011. I don't care to defend Cameron's use of the phrase, but it seems to me that in its original context it was entirely in keeping with Winner's un-PC persona, it was funny and memorable partly for that reason, and it was a good example of advertising not taking itself too seriously – and not being afraid to be a bit controversial.

Bibliography

This book is indebted in many ways to the works of others. Many have provided historical source material that I've retold to illustrate my themes. Some have provided evidence and theories which I've tried to build on, and I'm grateful to these for having done much of the heavy lifting for me. Some contain detailed explorations of themes I could only touch on briefly. Others have offered ideas that I've chosen to take issue with, though I hope always in a spirit of respectful debate. My thanks go to all of them, and I only hope I've succeeded in adding something new to this continuing conversation.

Ambler, T. and Hollier, E. (2004). The Waste in Advertising is the Part that Works. *Journal of Advertising Research*, 44.4

Adams, B. (1997). *E Pluribus Barnum: The Great Showman and U.S. Popular Culture.* Minneapolis: University of Minnesota Press.

Anderson, A. (2000). *Snake Oil, Hustlers and Hambones: The American Medicine Show.* Jefferson, N.C.: McFarland & Company, Inc.

Arden, P. (2003). *It's Not How Good You Are, It's How Good You Want To Be.* London: Phaidon.

Argyris, C. and Schön, D. (1996). *Organizational Learning II: Theory, Method and Practice.* Reading, Mass: Addison Wesley.

Backer, B. (1993). *The Care and Feeding of Ideas*. New York: Times Books/ Random House.

Beckham, V. (2001). *Learning To Fly: The Autobiography*. London: Michael Joseph.

Belloc, H. (1906). 'The Singer', in *Hills and The Sea*. London: Methuen & Co.

Berger, P. and Luckmann, T. (1966/1991). *The Social Construction of Reality*. London: Penguin Books.

Bernays, E. (2005). *Propaganda: with an introduction by Mark Crispin Miller*. Brooklyn, NY: Ig Publishing.

Bernbach, W. (1980). Facts are not Enough. Paper from the 1980 Meeting of AAAA, May 14-18, White Sulphur Springs, West Virginia.

Bernbach, W. (n.d.) [ed. Willens,D.] *Bill Bernbach Said*. New York: DDB Needham.

Binet, L., and Carter, S. (2018). *How not to plan: 66 ways to screw it up*. Kibworth: Matador.

Binet, L., and Field, P. (2007). *Marketing in the Age of Accountability*. Henley-on-Thames: WARC.

Binet, L., and Field, P. (2013). *The Long and the Short of It: Balancing Short and Long-Term Marketing Strategies*. London: IPA.

Binet, L., and Field, P. (2017). *Media in Focus: Marketing Effectiveness in the Digital Era*. London: IPA.

Bonnange, C., and Thomas, C. (1987). *Don Juan ou Pavlov: Essai sur la communication publicitaire*. Paris: Éditions du Seuil.

Boorstin, D. (1961/1992). *The Image: A Guide to Pseudo-events in America*. New York: Vintage Books.

Borkowski, M. (2008). *The Fame Formula: How Hollywood's Fixers, Fakers and Star Makers Created the Celebrity Industry*. London: Sidgwick and Jackson.

Broadbent, S. (1999). *When to Advertise*. Henley-on-Thames: Admap Publications.

Bullmore, J. (1991). *Behind the Scenes in Advertising*. Henley-on-Thames: NTC Publications.

Bullmore, J. (2001). *Posh Spice and Persil*. (The 2nd Brands Lecture). Viewed on 2/9/20 https://www.britishbrandsgroup.org.uk/the-brands-lectures/

Bullmore, J. (2008). In Praise of Antinomies. *Market Leader*, 42, Autumn, pp.16-19. Viewed on 2/9/20 at https://www.marketingsociety.com/the-library/praise-antinomies

Carter, S. (2012). *John Webster: The Earth People's Adman*. London: DDB UK Ltd.

Catmull, E. (2014). *Creativity, Inc.: Overcoming the Unseen Forces that Stand in the Way of True Inspiration*. London: Bantam Press.

Cialdini, R. (1984). *Influence: The Psychology of Persuasion*. New York: Harper Collins.

City College of New York (2020), Branding and Integrated Communications Course Descriptions webpage, viewed 30/08/20, https://bic-ccny.org/program/curriculum/course-descriptions.

Clifton, R. (2009, ed.), *Brands and Branding (Second Edition)*. London: The Economist/Profile Books.

Cook, J.W. (2005, ed.). *The Colossal P.T. Barnum Reader*. Urbana, Ill: University of Illinois Press.

Cooper, C., Cook, L. and Jones, N. (1991). How the Chimps have kept PG Tips brand leader through 35 years of intense competition. Chapter 1 in *Advertising Works 6*, ed. Feldwick, P. pp.3-25. Henley-on-Thames: NTC Publications.

Cracknell, A. (2011). *The Real Mad Men*. London: Quercus.

Damasio, A. (1996). *Descartes' Error: Emotion, Reason and the Human Brain*. London: Papermac.

de Board, R. (1978). *The Psychoanalysis of Organizations*. London and New York: Routledge.

Delaney, S. (2007). *Get Smashed: The story of the men who made the adverts that changed our lives*. London: Sceptre.

Donaton, S. (2004). *Madison and Vine: Why the Entertainment and Advertising Industries Must Converge to Survive.* New York: McGraw-Hill.

Driver, J. and Foxall, G. (1984). *Advertising: Policy and Practice.* Eastbourne: Holt, Rinehart and Winston.

Earls, M. (2007). *Herd: How to Change Mass Behaviour by Harnessing Our True Nature.* Chichester: John Wylie and Sons.

Earls, M. (2015). *Copy, Copy, Copy.* Chichester: John Wiley and Sons.

Edmondson, A. (1999). Psychological Safety and learning behaviour in work teams. *Administrative Science Quarterly*, 44,2 (June), pp. 350-383.

Ereaut, G. (2012). Strategy and Discourse. Chapter 8 in Verity, J. (ed.) *The New Strategic Landscape: Innovative Perspectives on Strategy*, pp. 123-143. London: Cass Business Press/Palgrave Macmillan.

Ewen, S. (1996). *PR! A Social History of Spin.* New York: Basic Books.

Feldwick, P. (1996). Do we really need 'Brand Equity'? *Journal of Brand Management*, 4.1, pp.9-28.

Feldwick, P. (1997). Barclaycard – 'Put It Away Bough'. Chapter 15 in *Advertising Works 9*, ed. Duckworth, G., pp. 365-386. Henley-on-Thames: NTC Publications.

Feldwick, P. (1997b). The Defensive Role of Advertising. Chapter 12 in *Excellence in Advertising: The IPA Guide to Best Practice*, ed. Butterfield, L. Oxford: Butterworth-Heinemann.

Feldwick, P. (2002). *What Is Brand Equity, Anyway? Selected Papers on Brands and Advertising.* Henley-on-Thames: World Advertising Research Centre.

Feldwick, P. (2005). A True Story [Barclaycard]. *Market Leader*, Winter, pp. 30-33.

Feldwick, P. (2010). Video: Aesthetics, Jugs, and Rock and Roll. TEDx New Street, October 22. Viewed on 02/09/20 at https://www.youtube.com/watch?v=JDIdgE68Byc

Feldwick, P. (2012). *Coming Out To Play: The Everyday Experience of Creative Process.* Unpublished dissertation for MSc in Organisation Consulting, Ashridge Business School.

Feldwick, P. (2015). *The Anatomy of Humbug: How to Think Differently About Advertising*. Kibworth: Matador.

Feldwick, P. (2018). How Does Advertising Work? Chapter 10 in *The Advertising Handbook (Fourth Edition)*, ed. Hardy, J., Powell, H. and Macrury, I., pp. 165-174. London: Routledge.

Feldwick, P. (2018b). What I learnt from John Webster. Chapter 32 in Schneiders, W. (2018), pp. 256-259.

Feldwick, P. (2019). Brand experience should not distract marketers from fundamental brand truths. *Admap*, October. https://www.warc.com/newsandopinion/opinion/brand-experience-should-not-distract-marketers-from-fundamental-brand-truths/3239 viewed on 22/09/20

Field, P. (2019). *The Crisis in Creative Effectiveness*. London: IPA.

Fiske, J. (1989). *Understanding Popular Culture*. London: Routledge.

Fletcher, W. (2008). *Powers of Persuasion: The Inside Story of British Advertising 1951-2000*. Oxford: University Press.

Fox, S. (1990). *The Mirror Makers: A History of American Advertising*. London: Heinemann

Frank, T. (1997). *The Conquest of Cool: Business Culture, Counterculture, and the Rise of Hip Consumerism*. Chicago: University of Chicago Press.

Gardner, B. and Levy, S. (1955). The Product and the Brand. *Harvard Business Review*, March-April, pp.33-39.

Gladwell, M. (2000). *The Tipping Point: How Little Things Can Make a Big Difference*. Boston: Little, Brown and Company.

Gluckman, D. (2017). *"That S*it Will Never Sell": A book about ideas by the person who had them*. London: Prideaux Press.

Gossage, H. (1995). *The Book of Gossage*. Chicago: The Copy Workshop.

Harrison, S. (2020). *Can't Sell, Won't Sell: Advertising, Politics and Culture Wars; Why Adland has stopped selling and started saving the world*. (Second Edition). Adworld Press.

Heath, R. (2001). *The Hidden Power of Advertising*. Henley-on-Thames: Admap Publications.

Heath, R. (2012). *Seducing the Subconscious: The Psychology of Emotional Influence in Advertising*. Chichester: Wiley-Blackwell.

Heath, R. and Feldwick, P. (2008). Fifty Years Using the Wrong Model of Advertising. *International Journal of Market Research*, 50:1, pp. 29-59.

Hirschhorn, L. (1990). *The Workplace Within: Psychodynamics of Organizational Life*. Cambridge, Mass: The MIT Press.

Hoffman, B. (2017). *Bad Men: How Advertising Went from a Minor Annoyance to a Major Menace*. Type A Group, LLC.

Hoffman, B. (2018). The Devaluation of Creativity. Chapter 33 in Schneiders, W. (ed.). *Eat Your Greens: Fact-based thinking to improve your brand's health*. pp. 60-266. Kibworth: Matador.

Hoffman, B. (2019). The Problem With Bubba's Burgers. *The AdContrarian Newsletter* #185, November 24th. Retrieved from https://www. bobhoffmanswebsite.com/newsletters .

Holt, D. (2004). *How Brands Become Icons: The Principles of Cultural Branding*. Boston: Harvard Business School Press.

Holt, D. and Cameron, D. (2010). *Cultural Strategy: using innovative technologies to build breakthrough brands*. Oxford: University Press.

Hopkins, C. (1923 and 1927/1986). *Scientific Advertising* and *My Life in Advertising*. Chicago: NTC Business Books.

Imseng, D. (2016). *Ugly is Only Skin-Deep: The Story of the Ads That Changed the World*. Kibworth: Matador.

Isaacson, W. (2011). *Steve Jobs*. London: Little, Brown.

Jenkins, H. (2008). *Convergence Culture: Where Old and New Media Collide*. New York: University Press.

Johnson, S. (1759). The Art of Advertising Exemplified. *The Idler*, No 40. Saturday, January 20th. https://www.johnsonessays.com/the-idler/no-40-art-of-advertising/ viewed on 14/09/20.

Jones, J. (1992). *How Much Is Enough: Getting the Most from your Advertising Dollar*. Lexington, Mass: Lexington Books.

Jones, J. (1995). *When Ads Work: New Proof That Advertising Triggers Sales*. New York: Lexington Books.

Joubert, M. (2002). *challenging convention: creativity in organisations*. London: RSA.

Kahneman, D. (2011). *Thinking, fast and slow*. London: Allen Lane.

Kapferer, J-N.(1992). *Strategic Brand Management: New Approaches to Creating and Evaluating Brand Equity*. London: Kogan Page/ Les Editions de l'Organisation.

Kearon, J., Wood, O. and Ewing, T. (2017). *System1 : Unlocking Profitable Growth*. London: System1 Group plc.

Knight, P. (2016) *Shoe Dog*. London: Simon and Schuster.

Kucharski, A. (2020). *The Rules of Contagion: Why Things Spread – and Why They Stop*. London: Profile Books.

Lannon, J. and Baskin, M. (2007). *A Master Class in Brand Planning: The Timeless Works of Stephen King*. Chichester: John Wiley & Sons.

Lears, J. (1994). *Fables of Abundance: A Cultural History of Advertising in America*. New York: Basic Books.

Marquette, A. (1967). *Brands, Trademarks and Good Will: The Story of the Quaker Oats Company*. New York: McGraw Hill.

Margerum, E. (2002). The Case for Sunny Jim: An Advertising Legend Revisited. *Sextant*, XII: 2. Retrieved from http://www.salemstate.edu:80/sextant/volXII_2/SEXT-essay-sunny-jim.htm .

Martineau, P. (1957), *Motivation in Advertising: Motives that Make People Buy*. New York: McGraw-Hill.

Mayer, M. (1958) *Madison Avenue, USA: the Inside Story of American Advertising*. London: The Bodley Head.

McGilchrist, I. (2009). *The Master and his Emissary: The Divided Brain and the Making of the Western World*. New Haven: Yale University Press.

McNamara, B. (1995). *Step Right Up*. Jackson: University Press of Mississippi.

McQueen, A. (2011). *The King of Sunlight: How William Lever cleaned up the world*. London: Corgi.

Menzies, I. (1970). *The functioning of Social Systems as a Defence Against Anxiety*. London: The Tavistock Institute of Human Relations.

Milligan, A. (2004). *Brand It Like Beckham: The Story of How Brand Beckham Was Built*. London: Cyan Books.

Morton, A. (2000). *Posh & Becks*. London: Michael O'Mara Books.

Murphy, J. (2017). *Brandfather: The Man Who Invented Branding*. Kibworth: The Book Guild Ltd.

Norwich, J. (1981). *A History of Venice*. London: Penguin

Ogilvy, D. (1963/2013). *Confessions of an Advertising Man*. Harpenden: Southbank Publishing.

Ogilvy, D. (1983). *Ogilvy on Advertising*. London: Pan Books.

Packard, V. (1957). *The Hidden Persuaders: An Introduction to the techniques of mass-persuasion through the unconscious*. London: Longmans, Green & Co.

Pendergrast, M. (1993). *For God, Country and Coca-Cola: The Unauthorized History of the World's Most Popular Soft Drink*. London: George Weidenfeld and Nicholson.

Pritchard, E. (2017). *Where Did It All Go Wrong? Adventures at the Dunning-Kruger peak of advertising*. P&D CreateSpace Independent Publishing.

Reeves, R. (1961/1986). *Reality in Advertising (sixteenth printing)*. New York: Alfred A. Knopf.

Ries, A. and Trout, J. (2001, reprint). *Positioning: The Battle for Your Mind*. New York: McGraw-Hill

Romaniuk, J. (2018). *Building Distinctive Brand Assets*. Sydney: Oxford University Press.

Rutherford, P. (2018). *The Adman's Dilemma from Barnum to Trump*. Toronto: University of Toronto Press.

Samuel, L. (2010). *Freud on Madison Avenue: Motivation research and Subliminal*

Advertising in America. Philadelphia: University of Pennsylvania Press.

Sayers, D. (1933). *Murder Must Advertise: A Detective Story*. London: Gollancz

Saxon, A. (1989). *P.T.Barnum: The Legend and The Man*. New York: University of Columbia Press.

Schneiders, W. (2018, ed.). *Eat Your Greens: Fact-based thinking to improve your brand's health*. Kibworth: Matador.

Schön, D. (1991). *The Reflective Practitioner: How Professionals Think in Action*. Aldershot: Ashgate.

Schultze. Q. (1983). The origins of university-level advertising instruction in the United States, 1900-1917. *Journal of Advertising History*, Number 7 (October), pp.10-13.

Scott, W. (1903/1921). *The Psychology of Advertising in Theory and Practice*. Boston: Small, Maynard & Co.

Sharp, B. (2010). *How Brands Grow: What Marketers Don't Know*. South Melbourne: Oxford University Press.

Sontag, S. (1966/2009). *Against Interpretation and Other Essays*. London: Penguin Modern Classics.

Stacey, R. (2011). *Strategic Management and Organisational Dynamics: The Challenge of Complexity*. Harlow: Financial Times Prentice Hall.

Standage, T. (2013). Social Media: It's So 1st Century BC. *Los Angeles Times*, Oct 27th.

Sternberg, R. (1999). (ed.) *Handbook of Creativity*. Cambridge: University Press.

Thompson, D. (2017). *Hit Makers: How Things Become Popular*. London: Allen Lane.

Wakeman, F. (1946). *The Hucksters*. New York: Rinehart & Company, Inc.

Watzlawick, P., Bavelas, J. and Jackson, D. (1967). *Pragmatics of Human Communication*. New York: W.W.Norton & Co.

Willens, D. (2009). *Nobody's Perfect: Bill Bernbach and the Golden Age of Advertising*. New York(?): CreateSpace.

Williams, R. (1976). *Keywords: A Vocabulary of Culture and Society.* London: Fontana/Croom Helm.

Wilson, T. (2002). *Strangers to Ourselves: Discovering the Adaptive Unconscious.* Cambridge, Mass: The Belknap Press of Harvard University Press.

Wood, O. (2019). *Lemon: How the Advertising Brain Turned Sour.* London: IPA.

Wu, T. (2016). *The Attention Merchants.* London: Atlantic Books.

Yakob, F. (2015). *Paid Attention: Innovative Advertising for a Digital World.* London: Kogan Page.

Zyman, S. (2002). *The End of Advertising As We Know It.* Hoboken, NJ: John Wiley & Sons, Inc.